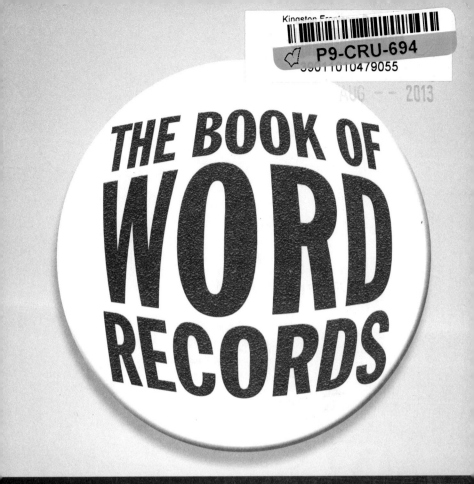

THE BOOK OF
WORD
RECORDS

A Look at Some of the Strangest, Shortest, Longest, and Overall Most Remarkable Words in the English Language

Asher Cantrell

adamsmedia
Avon, Massachusetts

Published by
Adams Media, a division of F+W Media, Inc.
57 Littlefield Street, Avon, MA 02322. U.S.A.
www.adamsmedia.com

ISBN 10: 1-4405-6330-6
ISBN 13: 978-1-4405-6330-0
eISBN 10: 1-4405-6331-4
eISBN 13: 978-1-4405-6331-7

Printed in the United States of America.

10 9 8 7 6 5 4 3 2 1

Many of the designations used by manufacturers and sellers to distinguish their
product are claimed as trademarks. Where those designations appear in this book
and F+W Media was aware of a trademark claim, the designations have been printed
with initial capital letters.

Cover credits © 123RF.COM/David Sandonato.

This book is available at quantity discounts for bulk purchases.
For information, please call 1-800-289-0963.

For my grandfathers, Benjamin J. Lisle and C. Thomas Cantrell. I wouldn't have done this without your constant encouragement.

Contents

Contents

Introduction

The greatest invention in human history is language. We didn't "invent" fire. Fire was already there, and we just figured out ways to control it. Sure, we came up with the wheel and tools and all of that stuff, and they've served us well, but eventually we had to come up with a way to pass on the methods for making wheels and tools, and for less tangible things, like warnings of danger. That's where language came in.

And, more than any other invention in our history, language has been the thing that makes us human. Being able to convey ideas and concepts to one another via simple, powerful sounds is how our culture survived, how our knowledge survived, and how we survived. Our strength is in our societies, and our societies grew strong because of words.

From language came writing, and from writing came the printing press, and from the printing press, we now have the Internet. Each iteration improves and reinforces our vast cultural knowledge, which, in turn, strengthens us as a society and, indeed, as a species. *Homo sapiens* have one thing no other animal before us has had: a network of information, millennia deep, that we keep encoded in our brains and express through voices and books. Every time you open your mouth, you are connected to your ancestors by a bond no other creature has.

As extraordinary as language is, though, we take it for granted. We tell our friends and family and coworkers the things they might want or need to know, ask questions about things we don't know, and create things that we'd like other people—strangers, even—to know. But how often do we truly celebrate language? How often do we say, "Gosh, I'm glad I'm able to express myself clearly and easily through an established vocabulary and the standard rules of grammar"?

That's what this book is about. We're looking at some of the biggest, the smallest, the longest, the shortest, and the weirdest things about our language. (Mostly English, since that's what you're reading right now.) We're parading around the great and strange things that we've done with nothing more than our minds and our words, because they deserve to be celebrated. If we can't spend all of our time marveling at the concept of language itself, the least we can do is commemorate the record-breaking uses of it.

All right, that's enough abject seriousness from all of us, your humble compilers of this tome you now hold. From here on, we promise to spice things up with the occasional, well-timed joke and what-have-you. Enjoy these mind-blowing words, phrases, books, albums, stories, puzzles, games, and whatever else we manage to find and toss in here. We promise only the best.

Twelve

of the
Most Popular
Passwords
(and Why They're Awful)

Computer security sucks; there's no doubt about that. That's why businesses tend to pay people to take care of it for them. Unfortunately for us regular people, that's not really an option. You can try bugging your family member who "knows about these things," but that only works a couple of times before they finally build an effigy of you and start sticking its head in their processor fan.

So it's up to you to figure it out for yourself, and that's where things fall apart. The average person knows somewhere between jack and crap about computer security, and that's how we've ended up with a world full of people running out-of-date antivirus software (or none at all) and choosing awful passwords like the ones below.

(For the record, computer security experts say that the strongest passwords are actually phrases made up of random common words separated by spaces, like "toaster mustache accent pistol," for example. They also happen to be much easier to remember than "Ge-&930!xq," or whatever, which is totally not our office mainframe password. We hope.)

These passwords aren't necessarily the most common passwords *ever* (since that tends to vary based on factors like the year, the age of the user, geographic location, etc.), but they are the ones that show up over and over in the databases of sites that get hacked. Whatever you do, don't set your password as . . .

12. "Princess" or "Dragon"

Apparently there are a lot of medieval fantasy fans roaming the Internet. Who knew? There's nothing wrong with getting down with some *Lord of the Rings* or *Game of Thrones*, but at least try to pick something that isn't one of the two defining characteristics of the genre. Hell, even *Shrek* is about a guy (ogre) saving a princess (ogre) from a dragon (with a donkey fetish).

Ask any five-year-old to describe a standard fantasy story and count how long it takes for them to get to either "princess" or "dragon." If you're a fantasy fan and a hacker knows it, that's how long it'll take them to figure your password out. Therefore, by our logic, a five-year-old could hack your password.

11. ■ "Sex"

Everyone does it. (Well, maybe not everyone, but a lot of people, anyway.) Also, everyone's here because of it, which is gross to think about, so just ignore that part.

Point is, it's on everybody's mind pretty often. It's not like ALF or Wham! or something. It's unlikely that you'll ever hear, "Hey, remember sex? Whatever happened to that?"

But maybe you just think *that highly* of sex. Maybe it's your favorite full-contact sport. But guess what? It's *everybody's favorite full-contact sport.* It's a rare bird indeed who says, "Sex? Nah. Tried it, didn't like it."

If you really think this is a unique, original password, we're wondering if your village elders know you've snuck a computer into the community, Jebediah.

10. ■ "Baseball" or "Football"

Hey, so you're a sports fan? That's great! All those teams and numbers and stuff should give you some great material for a password. And yet many people apparently don't bother in the slightest, and just go with the actual name of the sport they enjoy. That's like loving ice cream and also choosing "ice cream" as your favorite flavor.

Seriously, pick your favorite team or player and one of their records or some stats or something, then mash them together, and there's a password that's at least marginally better than just "baseball" or "football."

9. ■ "LetMeIn"

We don't know what's more disappointing—how terrible this password is, or the fact that they didn't say "please." *Talk about rude.* Machines have feelings, too, according to *Robocop*, *Terminator 2*, and *Battlestar Galactica*.

But still, who comes up with something like this, besides Ali Baba? At least he and the forty thieves had a kind of clever password. (Open Sesame, open says-a-me. Get it? It took us way too long to figure out.) "LetMeIn" is just lazy and kind of jerkish. It'd be nice if computers locked these people out of their accounts solely out of spite.

8. ■ "Monkey"

We get it, monkeys are cute and everything, but password-worthy? In a world of things like kittens and puppies and whatever baby sloths are called? We'll give you a minute to go search for baby sloth pictures on the Internet . . .

Back yet? They're adorable, right?

Anyway, you'd think people cared a lot more about other kinds of animals than monkeys, but apparently not. They're by far the most popular animal-related password.

Maybe it's because monkeys are inherently hilarious and people could use the laugh? Possibly. Taking it further, maybe there are some poor, desperate office drones for whom thinking of monkeys as often as they can is the only thing that gets them through the day without plunging out of the nearest window.

7. ■ Swear Words

Take any dirty four-letter word you can imagine (and probably some you don't want to) and you'll see it over and over in password databases. Presumably, it's because curse words are fun, easy to remember, and a lot of humans secretly have the mindset of a fifteen-year-old.

The only problem is that those words are in *everyone's* mental dictionary. Yes, your doting old grandma knows the f-word, even if you never, ever hear her say it, the Dalai Lama and the Pope *both* know about the c-word, and even beloved TV dad Alan Thicke is (presumably) aware that the n-word is a thing.

So not only are you using words that are familiar to 99 percent of the population, but you're also choosing the first words that are going to pop up into someone's head as soon as they get pissed off that they can't figure out your password.

6. ■ "God"

Despite what crazy, screaming people on TV would have you believe, the majority of people are still at least somewhat religious, even if they're a little lazier about making it to Sunday services (or Saturday temple) than they were when that was the only thing to do in town.

Maybe they're not open about their religion, but a lot of folks apparently trust the Big Guy enough to protect their online accounts. Sadly, it appears that He has other stuff on His mind besides keeping your credit card numbers safe. Maybe that's His way of telling you to put a little more forethought into your passwords.

5. "Ninja"

Maybe God's not your cup of tea, and you put your faith in a different kind of power—that of the mighty ninja, who will protect your account with katana and shuriken and badassery. While it's not a bad notion per se, it's obviously not going to help, as ninjas don't really care what your password is.

While the type of person who uses this as a password may think of himself as a badass ninja-type, *so do a lot of hackers.* And, as it happens, stealthily sneaking into things for the purposes of reconnaissance or causing havoc (all while keeping their identities a closely guarded secret) describes hackers a whole lot better than it does ninjas these days.

4. "Sunshine"

Well, hey, at least this one's nice and positive. And why not, considering most people use their computers indoors, probably in a cubicle where the nearest window is a football field away. People only use their laptops outdoors in commercials for erectile dysfunction, it seems, so it's probably nice to think about sunshine when you're stuck inside.

But so is everyone else around you, judging from how often this gets used. Turns out, humans are pretty partial to the sun. Like, we revolve around it, or something? Who knows, it could just be a terrible rumor, but it might be better to play it safe and get a better password.

3. ■ "ILoveYou"

Aww, isn't this sweet? We're sure your computer appreciates it and everything, but keep in mind that it is a cold, precise machine, and thus could never love a flawed human like you. Also, it's still mad at you for that time you tried to install the wrong printer drivers even after it warned you not to.

But seriously, this is such a common sentiment that it's one of the first things you learn in a foreign language, right around the time they teach you phrases like, "Where is your room of toilets? I have a heavy burden I must lay to rest." It's one of the first phrases kids pick up, if only because *they* already have a bathroom that follows them everywhere they go for the first couple of years of their lives.

It's found in basically every movie at some point, probably even *Rambo*. Actually, maybe not. But still, we have an *entire holiday* to celebrate love and expressions thereof. That's right, Columbus Day (Observed). He knew a lot about love and how to get it across the ocean and . . . oh, we've confused love and large, seafaring vessels again. Sorry about that.

2. ■ Strings of Consecutive Numbers or Letters

Finally, we've arrived into the realm of pure laziness. From this point on, we've left behind those who mistakenly choose bad passwords, and now arrive at the realm of people who just don't give a crap.

These are passwords such as "qwerty," "12345," "abc123," "abcdef," "696969," and numerous others like them. For the love of Steve Jobs, if you use a password like this for anything important, you probably have no business around computers whatsoever unless you're in a comedy and your password is the punch line to a joke.

1. ■ "Password"

Okay, we take that back. *This* is the password that's the punch line to a joke. It's like an Abbott and Costello routine.

"What's your password?"

"Password."

"Right, the code you use to unlock your computer."

"Password."

"Yeah, what is it?"

"Password!"

Unless you have some sort of disability where you can only remember the last thing you read, there's no valid reason to use this as your password.

But come on, this is the equivalent of leaving your password blank. You don't give a crap about security and you're not even pretending to. Do you leave your keys in the car and your house unlocked, too? If you do, well, uh, thanks for being consistent at least.

The Five Most Common PINs

With a four-digit bank PIN, there are only 10,000 possible numerical combinations to choose from. It sounds like a lot, but a computer trying each number iteratively would finish in just a few minutes. Most banks will kill your card after a few incorrect entries, but a smart thief will probably get three to five chances before that happens.

Obviously, the safest thing to do is make sure your card doesn't get lost or stolen. Barring that, though, just make sure you don't pick one of the numbers below. Computer security expert and data analyst

Nick Berry of DataGenetics.com got his hands on millions of previously leaked PINs, and these were the ones he saw the most.

5. **7777:** It might be awesome in Vegas, but it makes up just under 1 percent of all the PINs surveyed (meaning one out of every 100 if you missed percentages in school.)

4. **1212:** Not being able to count past two is never a virtue. This PIN was found to be approximately 1.2 percent of the total.

3. **0000:** Okay, did you fall asleep on the PIN pad? Because they'll let you pick another. It's okay. Also, talk to your doctor. 0000 covered nearly 1.9 percent of all PINs.

2. **1111:** You probably think you're smarter than those dopes who pick 0000 (or any number repeated four times), but sadly, you are not. You share the same PIN with a whopping 6 percent of the population.

1. **1234:** You might as well keep your money in a sock buried in a local park, for all the good this PIN is doing you. At least you're in good company, because nearly *11 percent of people* have just stopped giving a damn right along with you.

The Fifteen Longest Words
in the Dictionary

What's more annoying than the guy at an office party who likes to throw out huge words like he's getting paid by the syllable? Nothing, that's what. But you know what you can do to ruin that guy's night? *Make him look stupid.* Throw out some of these gigantic, beastly words, and watch your hipster coworker shrivel like his organic compost pile on a hot day.

But before you go and do that, there's one important step: *You have to know what they mean.* If your nemesis senses that you don't actually know the meanings of the words, this plan *will* backfire. Nothing makes a jerk like that more smug than the ability to distract you with other, unrelated intellectual boasts. Luckily, you've got this book on your side. And, because anyone can make up a BS word (and chances are that your rival would call you on that in a second), all of these words are in actual, scholarly dictionaries.

Important note: This is fighting fire with fire. You are not cool for knowing these words. You're just making yourself into a bigger jerk to highlight someone else's jerkishness. You might get some gratitude for shutting them up, but you almost definitely won't have anyone going home with you for the night.

15. Immunoelectrophoretically -adv.
(*im-yoo-no-ee-leck-tro-for-et-ick-ly*), 25 letters

WHAT IT MEANS: If you thought this list was going to be made of anything other than long, impenetrable medical terms, well, you should have known better. Be prepared to not know what any of this crap is.

Immunoelectrophoretically, the adverb form of immunoelectrophoresis, is the process of characterizing and separating proteins using electrophoresis (itself a process of moving particles around in a fluid by way of electricity) and antibodies (the things in your body that fight off germs and such; hence the "immuno-" bit).

Or, to put it more simply, it's kind of like looking for (and eventually retrieving) a needle in a haystack, except you have a giant magnet and an army of ferrets helping you.

A SAMPLE SENTENCE: "So, my buddies and I were in the lab and we had a bet going on that we could take Sam's blood and immunoelectrophoretically separate out the alcohol to find out how wasted he was. (He was completely wasted.)"

14. Psychophysicotherapeutics -n.
(*sy-ko-fiz-ick-ko-thair-a-pyoo-ticks*), 25 letters

WHAT IT MEANS: A branch of medicine that treats both the mind and the body. Although Eastern medicine hit on the idea that the mind and body could have an effect on each other back around the tenth century, the West only took *another 900 years* to come around. Psychophysicotherapeutics was an early term for what we now refer to as psychosomatic medicine. It's most famous for briefly appearing in James Joyce's *Ulysses*, which is a book that's filled with insane words that no one had heard of before that crazy Irishman dug them out of some linguistic subbasement. (That's not even considering *Finnegans Wake*, where he stopped even trying to make sense.) Even Shakespeare could look at Joyce's books and say, "What the hell is your problem, man?"

A SAMPLE SENTENCE: "My great-great-great-grandfather was a pioneer in psychophysicotherapeutics, at least until he tried to test his theories on a bear and found that not having a throat or face really doesn't do favors for your medical career."

How Many Words Are in the English Language, Anyway?

Rare, enormous words are great, but naturally they're not in anyone's everyday vocabulary. Even in the best cases, they're highly technical and not terribly conversational, as our sample sentences have probably proven. Obviously, they're outliers. The lint in English's bellybutton, as it were.

There are, of course, the everyday words, too (several of which we'll go over later in the book), but there's a whole lot of stuff in between. Just how many words are there in the English language?

According to *Oxford English Dictionaries* (our dictionary crush), the answer is a surprisingly low 750,000 words (approximately). Words, unlike stars, are apparently not infinite. For something as important to our everyday lives as language, you'd expect it to encompass some much larger number of individual components, but no, not really.

Everything from *Beowulf* to *Animal House* has been written with a toolbox of less than a million pieces. To make things even more mind-blowing, the average human only knows about 15,000 words. That may sound like a lot, but if you were to list them all, it'd still be shorter than this book.

Of course, we're allowed to reuse words as necessary (which is good, because we plan to talk about words *a lot*) and you wouldn't in a list, so it's not exactly the same, but it's enough that we feel confident in taunting you in a sing-songy voice and making up gross-sounding insult variations on your name.

13. Thyroparathyroidectomized -adj.
(*thy-ro-pa-ra-thy-roid-ec-to-mized*), 25 letters

WHAT IT MEANS: To have had both the thyroid and parathyroid glands removed. The thyroid, with which you're probably already familiar, is a gland that secretes hormones that allow the body to create proteins, expend energy, and control sensitivity to other hormones. When it goes bad, it screws up all of those things. So, if you see an overweight person, you shouldn't be rude to him or her, because he or she might just have thyroid problems (also because it's awful to be rude to people in general, and it's not cool to judge other people).

The parathyroid glands, on the other hand, are much smaller and are much more streamlined. Their entire job is to keep up with all the calcium in your body, like a sort of calcium accountant, and make sure it all goes to the right bones and such. Otherwise, it'd all end up on one side of your body and not the other, and you'd fall over a lot. Probably, anyway. We're not doctors.

A SAMPLE SENTENCE: "Due to the gamma radiation I received while trying to make myself into The Hulk, my thyroid and parathyroid reached critical mass and could take out a city block if they blew, so I was thyroparathyroidectomized by a team of surgeons in full hazmat gear."

12. Pneumoencephalographically -adv.
(*new-mo-en-sef-a-lo-graf-ick-lee*), 26 letters

WHAT IT MEANS: Having to do with an old-fashioned method of x-raying the brain by draining the cerebrospinal fluid and replacing it with oxygen or helium (so that your thoughts would be in a significantly higher pitch and make all the doctors laugh, probably).

It got discontinued later in the twentieth century for a simple reason: It caused unbelievable pain. Patients often experienced vomiting and extreme headaches (go figure). Also, they didn't just put your brain juice straight back into your head. You had to wait for your body to reproduce it normally, which could take several months. Nowadays, the procedure has been replaced by the much less painful and far more lying-in-a-space-tube-boring MRI.

A SAMPLE SENTENCE: "We pneumoencephalographically examined her brain, but instead of replacing the cerebrospinal fluid with oxygen, Simmons's jam sandwich somehow got stuck in there instead, and now we are wondering if the patient minds being called jam-for-brains."

11. Radioimmunoelectrophoresis -n.
(*ray-dee-oh-im-you-no-ee-leck-tro-for-ee-sis*), 26 letters

WHAT IT MEANS: Much like its aforementioned cousin, immunoelectrophoresis, radioimmunoelectrophoresis works along the same principals. It separates and categorizes proteins using electrophoresis, but instead of just using antibodies to aid in the process, it also tags the proteins using radioactive material.

To build on our previous metaphor, this is like looking for a needle in a haystack with a giant magnet and an army of ferrets, but the needle is now also glowing bright green.

A SAMPLE SENTENCE: "Even after immunoelectrophoretically examining Sam's blood, we still could not determine his exact level of intoxication, so we tried radioimmunoelectrophoresis instead; but something went terribly wrong and Sam turned into a radioactive monster."

10. Psychoneuroendocrinological -adj.
(sy-ko-nyoor-oh-en-doc-rin-oh-lodge-ick-al), 27 letters

WHAT IT MEANS: Having to do with the study of how hormones produced by the endocrine system affect the mind and behavior of an individual. Like how when you hit puberty you get all weird and moody for a couple of years—all those hormones turn you into a sullen brat.

Or, for the ladies, there are other examples, like PMS. When you hit that special time, your moods can get out of whack and provide all sorts of fodder for the terrible comedians that are your obnoxious coworkers and spouses. That's hormones. (And coworkers and spouses that probably need a good slap, because that crap hasn't been funny since the eighties.)

A SAMPLE SENTENCE: "According to my psychoneuroendocrinological research, premenstrual syndrome is directly correlated to women watching romantic comedies on the couch, eating ice cream, crying for no reason, and—ow, why are you bludgeoning me with that stapler?"

9. Electroencephalographically -adv.
(ee-leck-tro-en-sef-a-lo-graf-ick-a-lee), 27 letters

WHAT IT MEANS: Having to do with, or by, electroencephalography. Finally, a word you may know! Have you ever had an EEG? If not, you've probably seen a movie or TV show where they hook someone up to a computer and put electrodes all over their scalp.

Either way, that's electroencephalography, abbreviated to EEG. Electro, meaning electrical; encephalo, meaning head (like how someone who has "water on the brain" is hydrocephalic); and graph, meaning, you know, a graph. Thus, it is a graph of what's going on inside your melon, according to the electrodes stuck to it.

A SAMPLE SENTENCE: "I used to have these periods of missing time, so I went to the neurologist, got examined electroencephalographically, and they determined that I was actually posing as another person in my sleep."

8. Honorificabilitudinitatibus -n.
(*on-or-if-ick-ab-ill-it-ood-in-it-tat-ib-oos*), 27 letters

WHAT IT MEANS: To be able to achieve great honors. Technically, this isn't an English word at all. It's Latin, and the only reason it's in our dictionary is because of a man you may be familiar with named William Shakespeare. He loved dusting off old words and bringing them back as zombies.

Still, anything Shakespeare used automatically counts as an English word. If someone had written down what he sounded like when he was belching, you can bet that would be in the *Oxford English Dictionary* as well.

A SAMPLE SENTENCE: "Abraham Lincoln, Winston Churchill, Martin Luther King Jr., and Tom Hanks were all great, inspiring men capable of the highest honorificabilitudinitatibus, but only one of them won multiple Academy Awards and costarred with a volleyball."

7. Hepaticocholangiogastrostomy -n.
(*hep-at-tick-oh-co-lan-ge-oh-gas-tros-toe-me*), 28 letters

WHAT IT MEANS: An alternate/antiquated spelling of hepatocholangiogastrostomy (note the two-letter difference, as the latter is missing the "-ic-" in the "hepatico[. . .]" bit). They both mean the same thing, however, which is to ensure the proper function of the hepatic duct by, for example, clearing any possible blockages. So that you don't have to go scrambling for an encyclopedia, we'll go ahead and just tell you that the hepatic duct's job is to drain bile from the liver into the rest of the digestive tract. All together now: *Ewww!*

Naturally, if the hepatic ducts are not working or blocked, you've got a pretty big problem. No bile is flowing into your intestines, which will severely restrict (or even prohibit) digestion, as well as backing bile up into your liver. So it's an extremely important and sensitive procedure. (But also very gross.)

A SAMPLE SENTENCE: "My stomach was hurting very badly and I seemed to be having internal bleeding, so my doctor advised an emergency hepaticochol-angiogastrostomy, but he didn't have the necessary tools to perform the procedure, so he instead used a cleverly inserted twisty straw and a bicycle pump."

6. Spectrophotofluorometrically -adv.
(*speck-tro-foe-to-floor-oh-met-rick-lee*), 28 letters

WHAT IT MEANS: Having to do with the examination of the intensity of light in the entire spectrum of color given off by a fluorescent light. Okay, that probably didn't help. Let's try this: Using a device known as a spectrophoto-fluorometer (don't even worry about the name, just bear with us), each band of color in the spectrum (the colors of the rainbow) can be examined for its specific intensity. So if the red part of the spectrum is more intense, the light might give off a reddish tint, and the spectrophotofluorometer can tell you exactly how much more intense it is.

It sounds pretty useless outside of manufacturing light bulbs or bizarro quantum mechanics, but it's actually useful in medicine as well. Doctors have found, via some sort of wizardry that's not really necessary to explain for the purposes of this particular book, that it's very handy for accurately measuring the makeup of extremely small blood and tissue samples.

A SAMPLE SENTENCE: "We measured the light spectrophotofluorometrically and discovered that the problem was that there was actually a colony of microscopic humanoids that had somehow begun living there, and that they were very mad at us for bothering them, as evidenced by the fact that they were all simultaneously giving us the finger."

5. Antidisestablishmentarianism -n.
(*ant-eye-dis-es-tab-lish-mint-air-ee-in-is-um*), 28 letters

WHAT IT MEANS: You may have heard this one before as a popular example of the "longest word in English" (don't worry, we've still got a few more to go for that). It is also, thankfully, one of the very few non-scientific and non-medical words on this list.

This word refers to the process of disestablishment, which is what it's called when a country decides to no longer have an official religion, thus making it a secular state. Someone who is opposed to disestablishment would be antidisestablishment. You following us?

Although the word formed in response to a campaign to disestablish the Church of England back in the nineteenth century (which ended up not happening anyway), it's still valid today, as some critics of English politics are once again calling for disestablishment, while others (antidisestablismentarians, of course) are opposed to such a measure. Furthermore, evangelical religious groups in America have begun calling for "establishment"—that is, the creation of a state-sanctioned church in the United States, thus making themselves establishmentarians. There, don't you feel all politically informed?

A SAMPLE SENTENCE: "My cousin became involved in antidisestablishmentarianism, but decided he didn't like it that much when he found out that the plan was to later replace the state-sanctioned church with a cult that worships

Ronald McDonald, as he had once been thrown out of a McDonald's and was specifically told to 'Please leave our establishment.'"

4. Floccinaucinihilipilification -n.
(*flock-see-naw-see-nih-hill-ee-pill-ee-fick-a-shun*), 29 letters

WHAT IT MEANS: To describe something as worthless. Seriously. Much like our friend honorificabilitudinitatibus above, this is also a Latin loanword (of sorts), but we didn't get it from Shakespeare.

According to the most likely modern accounts, the word was probably coined as a joke by students at Eton College in the mid-1700s. The words *floccus* (a small piece of wool), *naucum* (a trifle), *nihili* (nothing), and *pili* (a single strand of hair) all appear in that exact order in the school's Latin textbooks from around that time.

So, you've got a bunch of words that can mean "worthless," some wiseass put them all together into one mega-word, and it somehow caught on and ended up making it into the dictionary.

A SAMPLE SENTENCE: "While trying to sell my homemade time machine, the salesman complained that it was worthless because of the deterministic nature of the cosmos, so I accused him of engaging in floccinaucinihilipilification for the sake of haggling me down to a lesser price, and he confessed that he had actually already purchased it tomorrow and was just using it today to get a better price yesterday."

3. Pseudopseudohypoparathyroidism -n.
(*sue-doe-sue-doe-hi-po-pair-ah-thigh-roid-is-um*), 30 letters

WHAT IT MEANS: To understand pseudopseudohypoparathyroidism, we must first understand its brother, pseudohypoparathyroidism (note that there's only one "pseudo" this time around), and to understand that, we need to first meet their dad, hypoparathyroidism.

As mentioned previously in the "thyroparathyroidectomized" entry, the parathyroid's whole deal is to direct your body's usage of calcium. Hypoparathyroidism is when the parathyroid doesn't produce enough hormone to do its job, and so the body loses calcium, thus making the bones very brittle (among other things).

Pseudo-hypoparathyroidism has a similar symptom (the body losing calcium), but the reason why is different. In this case, it's not the parathyroid's fault. The body is just resistant to the hormone the parathyroid produces, kind of like how becoming resistant to insulin is what gives you diabetes. To make things scarier, however, pseudohypoparathyroidism can occasionally result in skeletal defects.

Pseudo-pseudo-hypoparathyroidism throws yet another twist into the mix, like a horror movie that should have ended ten minutes ago. The sufferer has the skeletal defects that can result from pseudohypoparathyroidism, but their calcium level is normal, their parathyroid is working just fine, and they're not resistant to the hormone it produces. In this case, it's purely a genetic defect that just happens to resemble pseudohypoparathyroidism, hence the pseudo-pseudo. Confused yet? Excellent!

A SAMPLE SENTENCE: "I once had a coworker who was diagnosed with pseudopseudohypoparathyroidism, but it turned out that it wasn't genetic at all and was the result of alien experimentation that occurred during an abduction in his youth, which meant that he was the first person in history diagnosed with pseudopseudopseudohypoparathyroidism, also known as We Don't Know What the Hell's Going On Anymore Disease."

2.■ Hepaticocholangiocholecystenterostomy -n.
(*hep-at-ick-oh-co-lan-gee-oh-ko-lee-sis-ten-ter-oh-sto-mee*), 37 letters

WHAT IT MEANS: Remember hepaticocholangiogastrostomy from earlier? Meet its bigger, scarier colleague. It, too, involves the hepatic duct, but in this particular case, a hepaticocholangiocholecystenterostomy is a surgical procedure in which the doctor creates an artificial bile duct between the liver and the rest of the digestive tract, usually because the originals are too damaged to keep working.

Hepaticocholangiocholecystenterostomy is also notable in that it's frequently and specifically called out by medical professionals and scientists for being an example of medical terminology gone berserk. You see, doctors really want their patients to understand what in the hell they're talking about, and jargon like this (and other words found on this very list) are examples of exactly what they're trying to avoid.

A SAMPLE SENTENCE: "After my friends got tired of me constantly complaining and criticizing things, they told me they were 'sick of all my bile,' so I attempted to remove my bile ducts with a strategically placed vacuum cleaner hose, but all that did was ensure that I would need multiple hepaticocholangiocholecystenterostomies, and also to take things less literally."

1.■ Pneumonoultramicroscopicsilicovolcanoconiosis
-n. (*noo-mon-oh-ul-tra-mike-ro-skop-ick-sil-ick-oh-vol-can-oh-cone-ee-oh-sis*), 45 letters

WHAT IT MEANS: This is it. This is the big poppa. To be fair, it's a made-up word, but at 45 letters, it's the longest word to appear in the *Oxford English Dictionary*, so we're counting it. As for the made-up part, we'll explain: Its creation was motivated solely by the desire to make the longest word in the English language.

Pneumonoultramicroscopicsilicovolcanoconiosis was dreamed up in 1935 by the National Puzzler's League for no other reason than pure literary penis envy. They wanted the longest word, and by God, they'd have it. So Everett L. Smith, the group's president, took a real, ordinary medical condition and created the monstrosity you see above.

As for what it actually means, pneumonoultramicroscopicsilicovolcanoconiosis is just a really fancy name for silicosis, a disease usually contracted by miners. You can even see part of it jammed in the middle there.

Essentially, miners working with silica (which gives us the little bagged crystals you find in new shoes) can, over time, inhale so much of the dust that it destroys their lungs. It's super sucky, like most of the diseases you can get from mining, and it can and does kill workers all over the world, usually by way of a follow-up infection with tuberculosis.

A SAMPLE SENTENCE: "My cousin went on a trip to China and toured a silica mine where he ended up catching a very bad case of pneumonoultramicroscopicsilicovolcanoconiosis, but at least the gift shop was nice."

?? Methionylthreonylthreonylglutaminylarginyltyrosylglutamylserylleu . . . -n. (???), 189,819 letters

WHAT IT MEANS: Hey, what are you still doing here? Wait, none of those words shut the obnoxious coworker up? Not even pneumonoultramicroscopicsilicovolcanoconiosis? Okay, look, we shouldn't even be telling you about this, but . . . there's one more thing you can try. This is the nuclear bomb of words. It's not just the longest word in English. It's the longest word in *any* language. There's no coming back from this one. If you use it, we guarantee no one will be left in the room by the time you're done.

For this, we have to go outside the dictionary. That's right, leave your comfy reference books behind. We're going into no man's land. We're diving headfirst into *genetics*.

You should also know that you'll have to find this word on your own. That's just the first 65 letters up there. Printing it here would take up way too much space, because this word is an astounding *189,819 letters long*. For reference, that's slightly longer than *Hamlet*—a *single word* that's longer than one of the greatest pieces of writing in the English language. If you were to print it using a 12-point Times New Roman font, it would take *51 pages*. In November 2011, Dmitry Golubovskiy, an editor of *Esquire*'s Russian edition, released a video of himself reading it aloud. It took him three and a half hours (over multiple takes, no less).

As for its specific definition, it's the official chemical name of titin, the longest protein strand in the human body. Seeing as it's the longest protein, someone who hates language and probably also hates you, specifically, thought it would be cute to give it a stupidly long name. (Joke's on them, though, because that means they actually had to write it all down.)

Now, as a protein, it's actually very useful. It gives our muscles their passive elasticity that we need to move. As a word, however, it's only useful for trivia and showing how bored you were in your semester of Chem 101.

A SAMPLE SENTENCE: No. Don't even try it. Look, at this point, you're not even aiming to look like you're anything but a complete jackass. Just take a deep breath and start shouting it. By the time you're done, the party will be over, or you'll be unconscious from the effort. Either way, you won.

How an Oxford Editor Screwed Up the Dictionary for Forty Years

The *Oxford English Dictionary* is the most comprehensive dictionary ever made, and we are huge fans of it. Not only does it have contemporary and commonly used words like every other dictionary on earth, but it also includes hundreds of thousands of archaic and rare words, including foreign loanwords.

What's more, Oxford *never* deletes words from its dictionaries. Once it's put in there, it's in there forever, which is one of the reasons the dictionary is so massive. (The edition we used for research in this book was *twenty volumes long*, for example.)

Or, at least, that's the company line. It was discovered in 2012 that a former editor, Robert Burchfield, had, between 1972 and 1986, surreptitiously removed hundreds of words from the dictionary, primarily foreign loanwords. Strangely, Burchfield had accused former editors of being Anglocentric and pledged to open up the dictionary to more foreign words, all while he himself was covertly deleting 17 percent of the foreign loanwords included in the *OED*.

Current information points to him possibly being a racist, but we'll never really know for sure what his impetus was, since he died in 2004. Oxford has since pledged to re-evaluate all the words from previous editions that Burchfield removed in later ones. So no one panic, because we're sure you totally were.

Words

That Just Might

Win You a Game

of Scrabble

No book on words is complete without Scrabble. It's the most popular dictionary-based game of all time, short of a rousing game of "how many dirty words have dictionary entries?"

It's reportedly found in approximately one-third of American homes, making it more popular than toilet paper in some areas of the country. Also, it was created by a guy named Butts, which is more than you can say for . . . well, pretty much anything besides that old Seymore Butts joke.

The Highest-Scoring Scrabble Word

You're not here to mess around. We get that. Let's get to the big guns first. You want to know which Scrabble word will let you dominate your opponent and ascend the Throne of the Nerd Kings to begin your long reign.

Now, popular belief is that the highest scoring word in all of Scrabble is "benzoxycamphors," a fifteen-letter word that's worth forty-five points (not counting any bonuses) and requires at least eight of the necessary tiles to be already be on the board. But there's a big problem with that: Find that word in any dictionary. We dare you to try, because we couldn't. It seems to be an urban legend propagated through the Internet. It's not a real word, and not tournament legal.

Several websites give a definition of something like: "A type of chemical and also the longest word in Scrabble." What type of chemical? No one knows. No science or medical texts use it. Its only references seem to be about its prowess in Scrabble.

Even still, the highest-scoring word in Scrabble isn't easy to pin down. The two main contenders are also fifteen-letter words, "sesquioxidizing" and "oxyphenbutazone," worth forty-two and forty-one points, respectively.

But sesquioxidizing isn't technically in the dictionary, being a derivative of sesquioxide (which is a chemistry term referring to a certain kind of oxide). It's a real word, but it's not considered a legal move under U.S. tournament rules since it isn't in the Official Scrabble Tournament Word List. It is, however, a valid word under some British tournament rules (since they invented the language, they apparently get their own rules), which allow for derived words with a common suffix (i.e., -ed, -ing) that don't appear in the dictionary.

That leaves oxyphenbutazone, the scientific name for an anti-inflammatory drug, which is a real word and is tournament legal *everywhere.* It's only worth one point less than sesquioxidizing, which doesn't sound like a big deal, but players have calculated that under perfectly ideal conditions, oxyphenbutazone could rack up 1,780 points in a single play, whereas playing sesquioxidizing could potentially bring in up to *2,044 points.* Take *that,* America.

How to Perform the 2,044-Point Scrabble Move (Or, You Will Never Be This Lucky)

Arian Smit, a poster/writer who goes under the name "Asmit" on Scrabulizer, a congregation point for some of the biggest Scrabble nerds on the Internet, discovered this 2,044-point move in 2008 and it remains the highest-scoring Scrabble move found to this day. (Keep in mind, it's usually not tournament legal and nearly impossible to pull off, so don't start planning to destroy your friends with it.)

The move only requires that you or your opponent lay out a couple of other obscenely long words like "jabberwock," "overcompensate," and "portmanteau," which you then follow up by laying "sesquioxidizing" down the far-right side, with the s making "jabberwocks," the d forming "overcompensated," and the *x* creating "portmanteaux." It sounds confusing, we know, and there's a lot more to it, so why don't we just show you?

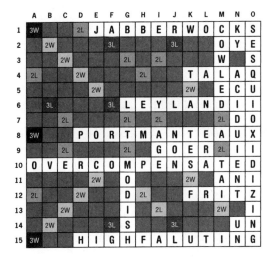

So you not only have to have "DGQSZXI" on your rack, but you also have to have the extremely unlikely situation pictured above before you can even lay "sesquioxidizing" down. Good luck finding someone who knows that you can even use "highfalutin" without a *g* on the end, and happens to play it in the right spot.

The Shortest Scrabble Words That Are Worth the Most Points

They say size isn't everything, it's what you do with what you've got. Probably the person who said that is just lying to you to make you feel better, but in Scrabble it's actually true. You can get a whole lot of points out of some very tiny two- and three-letter words.

There are obvious ones, like "ax" and "ox," and then there are these obscure, esoteric ones that you can use to really lay the hammer down. Also, we threw in the definition in case your opponent thinks you're just making crap up.

12. Jo -n. (*joh*), 9 points

WHAT IT MEANS: A Scottish term of endearment, basically meaning "sweetheart" or "darling." It was originally "joy," but since Scottish people speak their own variety of English, it slowly transformed into "jo" over the last 500 years.

Players using British rules can also toss out *ja*, the German word for "yes." It's worth the same amount of points, but it's not legal in American play.

A SAMPLE SENTENCE: "My jo went shopping and never came back; a few weeks later I saw a woman who looked exactly like her, but she said she was just an identical twin sister with the same name . . ."

11. Xi -n. (*zai*), 9 points

WHAT IT MEANS: The transliterated spelling of the fourteenth letter of the Greek alphabet, which is not to be confused with chi, the symbol of which the Romans shamelessly ripped off for the Latin letter *x*. The symbol of xi doesn't go completely unused in the English-speaking world, however, as it's used in several mathematical and scientific formulae.

Also, although Rome jacked the symbol from an entirely different letter, they still did sort of steal the pronunciation of *x* from xi, as it makes a sort of "ks" noise.

A SAMPLE SENTENCE: "My brothers and I in Xi Xi Xi see it as our solemn and humble duty to inform you that your face appears to be on fire."

10. **Xu** -n. (*soo*), 9 points

WHAT IT MEANS: A depreciated form of Vietnamese currency. At one time, 100 xu made up one dong (yes, Vietnam has the most hilarious currency ever if you still have a fifteen-year-old mindset). In more recent decades, however, inflation has caused the xu to be removed from circulation and the dong is instead used in both coin (for small denominations) and bill form (for larger denominations, currently up to 500,000 dong).

A SAMPLE SENTENCE: "My Vietnamese grandfather converted all of his money into xu so he could swim in it like Scrooge McDuck, but he never changed it back and now he's broke."

9. **Qi** -n. (*chee* or *chey*), 11 points

WHAT IT MEANS: It's an alternate spelling for chi, the mystical life force that flows through everything in Chinese culture, folklore, and religions. It's well known to Westerners, especially thanks to martial arts films and shows.

If, for some reason, you're not familiar with chi, just know that George Lucas based The Force pretty heavily on it (only with telekinesis and lightning and stuff added). In fact, ideas like chi tend to be pretty global. Unified spiritual and natural forces make appearances in dozens of Eastern belief systems and even some Western ones as well.

A SAMPLE SENTENCE: "Look, focusing your qi in order to play video games better does not make you a 'practitioner of Eastern religions.'"

8. ▪ **Zo** -n. (*zew*), 11 points

WHAT IT MEANS: A crossbred cow/yak hybrid found in Tibet, also called a Dzo. It's not some monster of genetic engineering; they're just able to breed with each other, producing a creature that is mightier than either of them, which is just what movies have told us should happen when species interbreed.

Unfortunately, this word is off-limits to American players in tournament play, but there is still Za, a contemporary slang term for pizza, that's worth the same number of points (don't worry, England, you guys can play that one, too).

A SAMPLE SENTENCE: "My zo petting zoo, The Zo Zoo, ended disastrously when people lined up around the block mistakenly thinking they'd be petting Zooey Deschanel."

7. ▪ **Kex** -n. (*kecks*), 14 points

WHAT IT MEANS: The dry, hollow stalk of certain kinds of plants, kind of like a reed. Generally speaking, this only applies to umbelliferous plants, such as carrots, celery, parsley, cumin, dill, and *freaking hemlock*.

In modern usage, the word has just come to refer to plants that have such a stalk, a general word for weeds, or even just a word meaning "a dry covering." Even still, that usage is pretty much limited to small geographical areas of England.

A SAMPLE SENTENCE: "My all-new, all-natural unisex undergarments are made completely from dried kex and now feature 17 percent less itching than before!"

6. Fez -n. (*fezz*), 15 points

WHAT IT MEANS: One of those little cylindrical hats with a tassel on top. (Yes, The Doctor from *Doctor Who* wears one sometimes, before we get a bunch of letters about it.) You've almost certainly seen one, even if you didn't know what they were called. Shriners often wear them, and they were visual shorthand for the Middle East in classic films (and Indiana Jones).

What you may not know is that for a few decades in the 1800s, the fez replaced the turban as the headwear of choice for people in the Muslim world, at least until most of the manufacturers moved to Austria. After a political spat, the manufacturers were boycotted for a year, which led to the fez falling out of favor. By that time, though, they had become fashionable as "smoking hats" in the West, and so the fez lives on today.

(Also, for the record, fiz is a similar word worth 15 points, but it's just an old-fashioned spelling of fizz, and that's not very interesting.)

A SAMPLE SENTENCE: "Listen, baby, I have something to ask you, and it's pretty weird, and if you don't like it, we totally don't have to do it, but just hear me out, because sometimes I like to wear a fez when I'm in bed. . . ."

5. Pyx -n. (*picks*), 15 points

WHAT IT MEANS: The box that communion bread or wafers for the Eucharist are stored in when they're being transported or not currently in use.

On some occasions, priests will take communion bread and wine out to those too sick to attend services, making it sort of like a doggy bag, but much fancier.

Technically, pyx can refer to any kind of box at all, as it comes from the Greek word *pyxis*, which means—you guessed it—box. In fact, the British Royal Mint has a tradition known as the Trial of the Pyx that dates from the Middle Ages, in which a selection of sample coins are placed in a pyx and inspected for quality by a judge and jury once a year. Considering modern manufacture of coins is totally automated, however, it's basically pointless these days and done just for tradition's sake.

A SAMPLE SENTENCE: "I know for a fact that your son has tampered with the pyx, as the wafers for Holy Communion were replaced with Chips Ahoy and the sacramental wine with Mountain Dew."

4. ▪ Zek -n. (*zeck*), 16 points

WHAT IT MEANS: A Russian slang term for a labor camp prisoner. Essentially, if you were sent to the Gulag (the government agency that administered the labor camps) during the days of the USSR, you were a zek.

The word was shortened from the Russian word for prisoner, заключённый (which sounds something like "zek-a-loo-cho-nee," but don't worry about that), down to зак, or zek. The term is still in use in modern Russia, but now it just means something more general, like jailbird or convict.

A SAMPLE SENTENCE: "I went to Russia for a week's vacation, but ended up a zek for a few days after I attempted to wrestle a bear I brought into Red Square in hopes that it would impress the Russian ladies. (It didn't.)"

3. ▪ Jiz -n. (*jazz*), 19 points

WHAT IT MEANS: Calm down, all of you who are snickering right now. It doesn't mean what you think. It's an old-fashioned term for a wig, also called a jasey or jazy. It most likely came from the word jersey, which in that day was a type of wool sweater worn by fishermen (on the Isle of Jersey, no less) as opposed to an athletic jersey.

The wig itself was also probably made out of wool, as human hair wigs were incredibly expensive. You probably needed your horses (if you had any) for other things, so horsehair was out of the question, and synthetic hair didn't really exist yet. You can imagine for yourself what it probably looked like, but we're betting it wasn't extremely flattering.

A SAMPLE SENTENCE: "Here, we have a 200-year-old jiz that was once worn by Ben Franklin after he burned his hair off playing with lightning."

2. ▪ Zax -n (*zacks*), 19 points

WHAT IT MEANS: A tool used for cutting or punching holes in roofing slate. It looks a bit like an elongated hammer. One end has a standard hammerhead, while the other contains a large pick for punching holes. On the bar that attaches to the handgrip, there's a large knife blade, used for cutting tile. Finally, perpendicular to the hammer/pick head is a crowbar for removing nails.

So it's like a hammer, a pickax, a crowbar, and a utility knife all had a baby, and yet, miraculously, *no one has used one of these in a horror movie to our knowledge.* Hollywood, get on the freaking ball.

Also worth noting is that those playing under British rules can also play the alternate spelling, zex, which is not a legal word in American play.

A SAMPLE SENTENCE: "I was working on a friend's roof a while back when my zax flew out of my hand, and by the time it reached the ground, it had hit fifteen people, started four fires, and called in fake bomb threats to six government buildings."

1. Zuz and Zzz -n. and intj. (*zooz* and *zee*), 21 points and 30 points

WHAT THEY MEAN: Before we get into definitions, we've got some bad news for you. These words are unplayable. They're valid words, part of the Scrabble word list in both American and British rules, but you can never play them, at least not at full points.

Why? Because there's only one *Z* in a Scrabble box, which is the whole reason it's worth so many points. Since both of these words have multiple *Z*s, the only way you can have them on the board is by using blank tiles, but those are worth zero points, which would make these only worth eleven points and ten points, respectively. For posterity's sake, though, let's go over them.

A Zuz is an ancient Jewish coin that was modified Roman currency. It originally featured Zeus (which may have led to its name). Since the Roman coins were made of silver, it was easy to restamp the coin with the design of the Zuz. What's more, the two coins were essentially interchangeable for this reason.

Zzz, meanwhile, is exactly what you think it is—a cartoonish way of depicting someone who's asleep and snoring. And while it would be awfully sweet to throw that one down on a triple word score one day, it's simply never going to happen. Sorry!

A SAMPLE SENTENCE: "I'm holding on to my *Z* in case I get another so I can play Zuz, or maybe two, and then I could play Zzz, or . . . oh, the game's over already?"

The Highest-Scoring Scrabble Game Ever

On October 12, 2006, the highest scoring Scrabble game in history was played. Obviously, this was worldwide news and the sky opened up and beautiful music poured out. (Yeah, absolutely none of that happened.) Still, it was one for the history books.

At the Lexington, Massachusetts, Scrabble Club, players Michael Cresta (a carpenter) and Wayne Yorra (a supermarket deli employee) played a simple game of Scrabble, not realizing they were about to change the world. (Okay, we'll quit with the hyperbole.)

They were just two average joes, enjoying a night off and playing their favorite game. Neither was a pro Scrabble*r* (both were ranked as "experienced novices"), and yet they played a 1,320 point game, with Cresta taking the win at *830 points*. Even Yorra's losing score of 490 was pretty freaking impressive.

Not only that, but Cresta also broke the record for the highest-scoring single move by laying down "quixotry" over two triple word spots, a double letter spot for X, and playing a bingo (using all the letters on your tray at once, which gives you an additional fifty points after your score is fully tallied). This gave him a huge 365-point play, the largest in Scrabble tournament history.

Eleven

of the
Longest Books
Ever Written

What's the longest book you've ever read? The last *Harry Potter* book? *The Stand*, perhaps? Maybe you even went for the big guns and grabbed *War and Peace* or *Atlas Shrugged* at some point in your life. Those are super-long books. You'd think they're somewhere in the top ten for the longest books ever written, right?

Not even close. *Harry Potter and the Deathly Hallows* is just under 200,000 words. *The Stand* adds up to over 450,000 for the uncut edition. *Atlas Shrugged* and *War and Peace* both clock in at about 550,000. The shortest book in our list is one *Harry Potter* finale longer than either of those. Make some space on your bookshelf for . . .

11. *Miss MacIntosh, My Darling,* Marguerite Young, 750,000 words

Begun in 1947, it took Marguerite Young nearly twenty years to write *Miss MacIntosh, My Darling*. Probably because she kept forgetting what the hell was going on. We'll explain: It's a dream-like novel that doesn't so much have a plot as a vague sequence of events.

Vera Cartwheel is riding on a bus to find her childhood nanny, Miss MacIntosh (who may or may not be dead), and begins to reminisce about her youth and the people who surrounded her during that time, such as her mother, an opium-addicted shut-in who spends her days holding conversations with dead people and inanimate objects.

For what it's worth, the book is regarded as either a masterpiece or a monstrous exercise in patience, as most editions of the book run about 1,200 pages and Vera doesn't even get off the bus until page 1,000 or so. If you're bored just hearing about it, at least you can buy a copy and probably sled with it or something.

10. *Romance of the Three Kingdoms,* Luo Guanzhong, 800,000 words

Romance of the Three Kingdoms is a fourteenth-century Chinese historical novel based on real events that occurred over 100 years during the second and third centuries A.D., including political intrigue, birth, sex, murder, and all things in between. Guanzhong is considered the Shakespeare of Chinese literature, and *Romance of the Three Kingdoms* is his masterpiece.

The story follows the collapse of the Han dynasty, and the war between three separate dynasties that laid claim to China and began a civil war in the years that followed. It's just like *Game of Thrones,* except this stuff really happened. Each warlord works against the others, and the stakes slowly shift and turn throughout the century, until one family finally rules a united China.

Oh, and that wasn't the last time this kind of thing happened in China, so it's probably pretty wise that Guanzhong started the book with its famous line: "All things divided under heaven will eventually be united and, after a time, those unions will once again divide."

Gadsby: The Longest Novel Without "E"

For some people, writing the longest novels isn't enough. They have to come up with ways to make it even harder on themselves. For example, in 1939 Ernest Vincent Wright wrote a 50,000 word novel titled *Gadsby* that doesn't use the letter *e* anywhere in the text. (For comparison, we've used it forty times in this very paragraph.)

The novel is the story of John Gadsby, a fifty-year-old man who decides to attempt to improve his city, Branton Hills, with a group of similarly minded youth. There's an actual story. Wright didn't just half-ass it. In fact, you can read it yourself and see, since the book is now in the public domain.

According to the author, the hardest parts were past-tense verbs that end with -*ed*, which led to him substituting common actions with *did* plus the word (like "did laugh" instead of "laughed"), and being unable to use any numerals between six and thirty. To ensure that he avoided *e*, he actually tied the key down on his typewriter, making it impossible to use at all.

The narrator even apologizes for his weird phrasing (blaming it on being a terrible writer) and acknowledges that he's trying not to use *e*, though he doesn't really give any particular reason why. Maybe his typewriter is broken, in which case we think we'd just get the freaking thing fixed first.

9. *Poor Fellow, My Country*, Xavier Herbert, 850,000 words

This one holds the specific record for the longest Australian novel ever written, which is great for our Aussie friends, because they need big books like this to crush those insanely huge spiders they have down there.

Set in the 1930s and 1940s, the book is a coming-of-age story of an Aboriginal boy named Prindy and explores the events and lives of those who surround him, including a cast of dozens of characters. Along the way, there's some fun social commentary about Australian life and how people shouldn't be jerks to each other, but that's just good sense.

Unfortunately, if you're wanting to read this one, you're going to have to lay down some dough. It's out of print and a little hard to find. Oh, and the fact that it's nearly 1,500 pages means it's probably not cheap to ship.

8. *Ponniyin Selvan*, Kalki Krishnamurthy, 900,000 words

Oh hey, it's another epic, sprawling historical novel about a particular geographical region and the people who inhabit it. Are we sensing a pattern? Apparently, if you want to write about the wars and politics of those who came before you, you'd better have a lot of paper on hand.

Ponniyin Selvan is a Tamil-language novel published throughout the 1950s in a series of five volumes. They are all a single novel, however, and were merely split up for the convenience of not having to wheel the book around on hand trucks (this will become a theme for the rest of this list).

The book tells the story of the Chola dynasty of India during the tenth and eleventh centuries. When Emperor Sundara Chola falls ill, various legitimate and not-so-legitimate heirs begin to make moves toward taking over the crown. It gets *way* complicated from there, with dozens of characters and storylines all interweaving before finally coming together about 2,400 pages later. But, to keep it concise, there's cyclones and assassins and bastard children and all kinds of other awesome, exciting stuff that every adventure needs.

If you happen to read Tamil, it's actually in the public domain in India. English translations do exist, naturally, but we can't guarantee that you won't have to shell out some cash for them.

7. *Clarissa*, Samuel Richardson, 1,000,000 words

Published in 1748 and typically collected in three volumes (note that some editions are a little shorter and come in under 1 million words), *Clarissa* is a tragedy that happens to be about a girl named Clarissa (because it'd be really weird if the book was called *Clarissa* and no one in it was named that). Clarissa is the youngest daughter of the Harlowe family, a nouveau riche clan hoping to score themselves a lord via marriage, because back then that was one of the only ways to make sure that each successive generation of your kids wouldn't eat dirt for their entire lives.

Clarissa decides that a good way to do that would be to marry Lovelace, the heir to an earldom. Her brother, James, objects and defeats Lovelace in a duel. Typical English literature so far, right? Except this is where everything goes crazy. Lovelace, angry at his defeat, *kidnaps and rapes Clarissa* in an attempt to force her to marry him, keeps her prisoner for months, and eventually causes her death from illness.

Basically, *Clarissa* looks at the word "tragedy" and laughs. There's no two ways about it—this is a depressing, disturbing book. Anyway, it's in the public domain if you're a total sadist and don't want to pay to read one million words about someone getting absolutely crapped on by life. *Damn.*

6. *Sironia, Texas*, Madison Cooper, 1,100,000 words

Released in 1952 and split into two volumes, *Sironia, Texas* is Madison Cooper's love/hate letter to small-town Texas. Living in Waco, Texas, for most of his life, it was a subject that Cooper was probably pretty familiar with.

Sironia, Texas doesn't have *a* plot. It has twenty-one of them. Around eighty different characters move in and out of each other's lives, often without realizing it, over two decades, from 1900 to 1921. The novel also covers themes like the death of southern aristocracy, small-town politics, racism, and the westward expansion of America.

Although the book was quite popular on its release, spending eleven weeks at the top of the *New York Times* bestseller list, it has since gone out of print and is now a bit of a rarity. Copies in good condition can go for hundreds of dollars for both volumes.

5. ▪ *Mission Earth*, L. Ron Hubbard, 1,200,000 words

Before he was famous for starting that religion that celebrities really like, L. Ron Hubbard was just a science fiction writer, and a fairly popular one at that. After Scientology started getting all the headlines, people mostly forgot about Hubbard's writing career, but he kept at it until his death. *Mission Earth*, his final novel, was split into ten volumes, but Hubbard only lived to see the first published (the rest were released posthumously).

The book tells the story of two Voltarians, Jettero Heller and Soltan Gris, the first an envoy sent to make sure the Earth stays in shape long enough to be conquered, and the second an alien CIA agent who becomes aware of a conspiracy involving Earth drugs and the highest echelons of Voltar leadership and tries to stop it.

It's meant to be a comedy, but that's a bit of a stretch considering it includes things like Soltan Gris (who is ostensibly the main character and hero) raping two lesbians to "cure" them and alleging that rock-and-roll music is a conspiracy to promote homosexuality. Oh, and the bad guys use psychology as a weapon, but that's kind of expected.

Boy, that L. Ron Hubbard sure was a *hilarious* guy, right? Or something, anyway. In actuality, the book is quite famous among science fiction critics as being—we're paraphrasing here—creepy and disgusting. (And terrible. Did we mention terrible?)

How Many Books Are There in the World?

These books obviously take up a lot of room on the shelf, but you can always buy more shelves, right? At least until you have no more space in your house and they all fall over and you suffocate in that pleasant book smell, anyway.

But let's say you weren't trying to set up a *Hoarders*-esque death trap and truly needed to know how many books were in the world, so you could buy enough shelves to house all of them.

That's the problem that Google ran into when they started their Google Books project. Because they pledged to scan every extant book in the entire world, they needed to know how big their database would have to be (to be able to easily index the books) and how much server space they'd require (to store all of those books in digital format).

Using various Google magic formulas (look, it may as well be magic that they know exactly what we're talking about when we type in "how to deal with a rude duck who maybe has a gun") and dozens of book catalogs from around the world, they were able to determine that, as of 2010, there were approximately *130 million books in the world*. And who knows how many we've added since then. (Besides Google. We assume they know.)

So if you ever felt up to the task of reading every book ever (keep in mind that you have to find some way to procure them because you're not an enormous Internet company), you could read ten every month and it would only take you . . . approximately 1,084,000 years. *Totally* doable, but only if you start right now. Don't forget to catch up on the stuff published in the million years since you started once you get to the end.

4. *L'Astrée*, Honoré d'Urfé, 1,400,000 words

You're about to learn a very important fact: French writers *love* writing gigantic novels. Of the final four novels on this list, three are by French authors, because apparently French people have a lot to write about. (Besides the beautiful countryside and amazing food, we guess.)

L'Astrée is broken up into six parts, the first three published between 1607 and 1619 and the final three (completed by other authors, as d'Urfé had died with them partially unfinished) in 1625 and 1626.

It tells the story of two sheep-herding lovers, Astrée and Céladon, and how their relationship is affected by those around them: family, friends, and various townspeople who mostly just cause trouble for the both of them. So it's *Every Serious Relationship You've Ever Had: The Novel.* Oh, and then occasionally it goes into completely unrelated stories, for some reason. Maybe to pad out that word count.

3. Remembrance of Things Past, Marcel Proust, 1,500,000 words

Remembrance of Things Past (or *In Search of Lost Time,* depending on the translation) by Marcel Proust (also known as "that guy who was a Monty Python punch line a few times") was published over the span of a decade and a half, from 1913 to 1927, and it remained unfinished at Proust's death. Of the seven volumes, the final three were reconstructed by his brother, Robert, from his notes after his death in 1922. So hey, it could have been a whole lot longer.

The book itself famously contains over *2,000 characters* and is a vague, not-quite autobiography of Proust himself and his youth and life in France. (The narrator/main character is mostly unnamed except for a throwaway line in the fifth volume identifying him as "Marcel.") In addition, it covers numerous philosophical themes like the nature of memory and the development of identity. It even has some pretty downright progressive and forward-thinking sections dealing with themes of homosexuality. So it's kind of the opposite of L. Ron Hubbard, at least in that regard.

2. *Artamène or Cyrus the Great*, Madeleine and Georges de Scudéry, 2,100,000 words

Artamène, another ten-volume monster, was written by brother and sister pair Madeleine and Georges de Scudéry and published over a period of five years, between 1648 to 1653, and holds the title for the longest book in French to this very day. And, in continuing with our theme of these books being either historical novels or thinly disguised philosophical tracts, *Artamène* is a swords-and-sandals epic set in Asia Minor during the time of Ancient Greece. (You can probably figure out which of those two genres this falls under.)

Artamène tells the story of Cyrus the Great, a real-life Prince of Persia (hopefully the acrobatic video game kind) and his conquest of the Asia Minor region. And it was all for a woman! *Swoon!* (Okay, in reality it wasn't that at all, but novels have to have the love angle, right?)

Cyrus's lady, Mandane, keeps getting kidnapped and Cyrus keeps trying to rescue her only to find that she's constantly being moved between various kings, causing Cyrus to conquer each kingdom . . . wait a second, that's the plot of *Super Mario Bros.*! Seriously, his princess is always in another castle and finally, once he's beat every king in the land, they're allowed to get together. All it really needs is a little mushroom person in each kingdom and sentient turtles.

1. *The Story of the Vivian Girls,* Henry Darger, 9,000,000 words

We've come to the end. The longest novel in the whole world, and it's not what you'd expect at all. *The Story of the Vivian Girls* is one of the most popular examples of outsider art (that is, people not connected to the art world—or writing world, in this case—in any way, who never study it, who still produce complex and original works, often just for themselves).

Henry Darger was a simple janitor from Chicago, but every night he would go home and work on his masterpiece: the story of a family of seven young girls and thousands of other children fighting an immense war against an entire population of atheistic child slavers. Over sixty years, Darger produced thousands of typewritten pages and even painted his own illustrations to go along with it.

The book was never published, and Darger never even told anyone it existed. All 9 million words of it were discovered by his landlord shortly before Darger's death. Little did he know that pieces of his life's work would go on to earn tens of thousands of dollars at auction, and become widely respected and studied in the worlds of both art and writing.

Two Even Longer "Novels" (And Why They Probably Don't Count)

Since the dawn of the Internet and eBooks, anyone can be a publisher, which means that writers can take even more risks and be even more experimental than ever before. Giant novels aren't a problem, because if they're eBooks, you don't have to carry them around anyway. It sounds pretty great, right?

As it happens, two writers have claimed to have written books even larger than those on this list, but we're not just being snobs by not including them. The first, *The Blah Story* by Nigel Tomm, clocks in at around 11 million words. Or, more specifically, a single word, "blah," repeated millions of times with a few random linking words peppered in. It's not exactly light summer reading.

The second is titled *Marienbad, My Love* by Mark Leach, who "wrote" an incredible *17 million words*. We put wrote in quotes for a reason, though, and not because it's mostly unintelligible. (So was *Finnegans Wake*, and that's considered a masterpiece.)

While the book is real and does contain 17 million words, not all of them are Leach's. Using a style that he dubbed a "cut-up method," Leach used an automated word mixer to create the book. He would dump paragraphs of text, sometimes his own, sometimes other works (he calls these "literary appropriations"), and sometimes just random snippets of whatever he felt was interesting, into the program and used the subsequent results as his book.

Essentially, the whole thing is a word puzzle created by a computer, while *The Blah Story* is like a *Mad Libs* book where every blank is filled with "blah." They're both fine as art pieces (maybe not even that, if you listen to their detractors), but do they count as novels?

We're not sure. They move into a gray area of redefining the idea of the novel itself. That's an argument we're staying out of because people will cut the nose right off your face over things like this, and we like our noses. Still, as far as experimental writing projects go, they're both cool and notable. As for the argument over their novel-hood, we recommend you find an unsuspecting web forum or YouTube comments page and scream at other people about it.

The Eight Longest Album Titles Ever

A good album title is a special thing. It should give you the tiniest hint of what you might find when you listen to it, but it can also give deeper meaning to an album you already love. If you say *Sgt. Pepper's Lonely Hearts Club Band* to a Beatles fan, his or her mind will immediately spit out a cherished memory of that record and also probably that really weird cover art.

The following musicians apparently decided that was stupid, and they never wanted anyone to mention their albums aloud, *ever.* What other explanation could there be for insanely long titles like . . .

8. ■ Cap'n Jazz, *Shmap'n Shmazz* (28 words)

FULL TITLE: *Burritos, Inspiration Point, Fork Balloon Sports, Cards in the Spokes, Automatic Biographies, Kites, Kung Fu, Trophies, Banana Peels We've Slipped On and Egg Shells We've Tippy Toed Over*

The first and only full-length release by '90s-era Chicago emo band Cap'n Jazz, this album is affectionately called *Shmap'n Shmazz* by fans. Honestly, can you blame them? It's like a to-do list for a mental patient with a weekend pass. Naming an album something like this has probably been added as a symptom of something in the DSM-5, right next to "is incapable of maintaining meaningful relationships without constantly picturing a breakfast cereal mascot."

As it happens, the longest song title on the album is only six words, so apparently they had to name their album the most unwieldy and ridiculous thing they could. Maybe it's code for a nuclear missile launch or something.

The album is currently out of print, though a compilation album, much more reasonably titled *Analphabetapolothology* (okay, relatively more reasonable), contains the band's entire catalog, *Shamp'n Shmazz* included.

7. ▪ Weird Wives, *Some Motherf*ckers . . .* (29 words)

FULL TITLE: *Some Motherf*ckers Gonna Be Walking 'Round With a Size 9 Diehard up Their Ass, Cause Apparently They Ain't Never Seen a Short AC Man Get Bad Ass on Methadone*

Weird Wives is a side project of West Palm Beach, Florida, band Surfer Blood. Typically a straightforward indie band, Weird Wives is the band's noise-rock alter ego (plus additional non-Surfer Blood member Nick Klein), because even nerdy guys in flannel need to cut loose and destroy an occasional eardrum. It's practically a requirement with ASCAP/BMI and the FCC.

Their 2010 debut album is named the above, and was reportedly inspired by a comment made by a pill-popping coworker at a construction job once held by Klein. And hell, when someone just hands you gold like that, what else are you supposed to do with it? Your choices at that point are to either name an album after it, or put it on a plaque and build a giant statue in that man's honor.

6. ▪ Lalo Schifrin, *Marquis de Sade* (30 words)

FULL TITLE: *The Dissection and Reconstruction of Music from the Past as Performed by the Inmates of Lalo Schifrin's Demented Ensemble as a Tribute to the Memory of the Marquis De Sade*

Argentinean composer Lalo Schifrin is the creator of numerous film and television scores. He's the guy who wrote the *Mission: Impossible* theme. (Yes, a mortal man wrote that and it didn't just create itself out of thin air, believe it or not.) Every time you forget to bring a towel into the bathroom when you take a shower and have to sneak around your house without giving your neighbors a peep show (or purposefully giving them one, if you're that kind of person), you're humming Lalo Schifrin's most famous work the entire time.

In 1966 Schifrin released this album, a collection of big band–style jazz songs based on the life of the Marquis de Sade (from whose name the word sadist was coined, because that idea didn't just create itself out of thin air, either, apparently).

More specifically, Schifrin based the album on a 1963 German play titled *The Persecution and Assassination of Jean-Paul Marat as Performed by the Inmates of the Asylum of Charenton Under the Direction of the Marquis de Sade*, itself a bizarre portrayal of de Sade's life in a mental institution. The parallels should be obvious. In the titles, we mean, not in the crazy sex pervert department.

5. ▪ Marnie Stern, *This Is It . . .* (31 words)

FULL TITLE: *This Is It and I Am It and You Are It and So Is That and He Is It and She Is It and It Is It and That Is That*

Experimental art rocker Marnie Stern's 2008 album is the last example on this list that, despite having a long title, is still of a not-totally-insane length. Enjoy it. You'll see what we mean soon.

Stern's second album, it was named one of the top 50 albums of 2008 by über-nerd music webzine *Pitchfork*. It features Stern's trademark crazy, extremely rapid style of playing, so it's almost like she picked a title that would take you so long to read, she could get a couple of riffs in while you were busy.

The title is a borrowed quote from twentieth-century British philosopher Alan Watts, who himself borrowed it from a poem by San Francisco poet/filmmaker James Broughton, and being a San Francisco poet in the 1960s, you can probably assume that, yes, he was One of Those Guys. (The drug ones, we mean.)

4. Premonition, *Look Into a Crystal Ball . . .* (79 words)

FULL TITLE: *Look Into a Crystal Ball and See That It's Kind of Like a Fairy Tale Between the Tides of Time and the Gates of Dawn, Where a Black Dove Flies Out of the Woods, a Mystical Wizard Casts His Spell Over the Land, a Shadow Hangs Over the Garden That Never Grows, and as the Dust and the Ashes Come Falling Down Like Rain, You Can Still Hear the Sound of Music, Forever Drifting Through the Winds of Eden*

Welcome to the other side. We've now entered the realms of madness. These album titles aren't even trying to be subtle anymore. They're just piles of words we're expected to sift through, hoping to find some kind of meaning. But maybe, just like life itself, there isn't one. Woe, discordia.

Sorry, we got existential there. Anyway, this album was the debut record from Nashville-based psychedelic band Premonition (a.k.a. Crystal Ball Premonition). The title is a free verse poem written by guitarist Cory Stuteville, and yes, the whole thing actually appeared on the cover of at least one edition of the album.

Later editions of the album were just referred to and labeled as *Look Into a Crystal Ball . . .* or simply *Premonition*, though the songs included remained the same. The album has since gone out of print due to the label, Xcessive Records, folding and the band going its separate ways. If you're interested, however, Stuteville's current band, The Dragon Cult, still plays some of Premonition's songs.

3. Fiona Apple, *When the Pawn Hits . . .* (90 words)

FULL TITLE: *When the Pawn Hits the Conflicts He Thinks like a King What He Knows Throws the Blows When He Goes to the Fight and He'll Win the Whole Thing 'fore He Enters the Ring There's No Body to Batter When Your Mind Is Your Might So When You Go Solo, You Hold Your*

Own Hand and Remember That Depth Is the Greatest of Heights and If You Know Where You Stand, Then You'll Know Where to Land and If You Fall It Won't Matter, Cuz You'll Know That You're Right

Long known to be a little on the weird side, Fiona Apple's second album was a ninety-word poem that she wrote in response to criticisms of herself and her music. The entire title was included as a clear sleeve that went around the outside of the disc's packaging, though the press usually referred to it as *When the Pawn Hits* . . . because they have other things to do.

The album was fairly successful, picking up a number of "best of the '90s" awards (which, in retrospect, is almost like a backhanded compliment). It even had three videos directed by Paul Thomas "I Drink Your Milkshake" Anderson, whom Apple was dating at the time. (Which one of the two do you think regrets that breakup more now? Critical darling film director who hooked up with Maya Rudolph from *SNL*, or critical darling musician who once got busted for drugs?)

Also worth mentioning is Apple's 2012 album, *The Idler Wheel Is Wiser Than the Driver of the Screw and Whipping Cords Will Serve You More Than Ropes Will Ever Do*, which, while much more succinct than *When the Pawn Hits* . . . , is still twenty-three words long and could have easily made number nine on this list.

2. Soulwax, *Most of the Remixes* . . . (103 words)

FULL TITLE: *Most of the Remixes We've Made for Other People over the Years Except for the One for Einstürzende Neubauten Because We Lost It and a Few We Didn't Think Sounded Good Enough or Just Didn't Fit in Length-Wise, but Including Some That Are Hard to Find Because Either People Forgot about Them or Simply Because They Haven't Been*

Released Yet, a Few We Really Love, One We Think Is Just OK, Some We Did for Free, Some We Did for Money, Some for Ourselves Without Permission and Some for Friends as Swaps but Never on Time and Always at Our Studio in Ghent

This record is a remix album by electronic artists Soulwax, featuring their reworkings of other bands' recordings (to be fair, they do have a whole lot of them), except for one they did for Einstürzende Neubauten, obviously. But you already knew that, didn't you? You're either psychic or patiently read that whole thing. Or good at guessing! (We guess it's the last one.)

Instead of a poem or extended quote, this title is just an incredibly verbose description of what can be found on the disc. It's handy if you're on the fence about buying it, we guess? It's practically an Amazon review in and of itself. If someone asked you what's on the album, you could tell them the title and by the time you were done, if they were still listening, they'd know.

The full title did, in fact, appear on the cover. As it happens, the title is so long that that's all that would even fit on the freaking cover. The effect is, essentially, the very definition of "wall of text." There's just barely enough room for the band name, squeezed up there into the upper right corner, like it's terrified of all the other words it got left with. It's okay, little Soulwax. You're bolder than them. You stand out. You've got this.

1. Chumbawumba, *The Boy Bands Have Won . . .*
■ (156 words)

FULL TITLE: *The Boy Bands Have Won, and All the Copyists and the Tribute Bands and the TV Talent Show Producers Have Won, If We Allow Our Culture to Be Shaped by Mimicry, Whether from Lack of Ideas or* *from Exaggerated Respect. You Should Never Try to Freeze Culture. What You Can Do Is Recycle That Culture. Take Your Older Brother's Hand-Me-Down Jacket and Re-Style It, Re-Fashion It to the Point Where It Becomes Your Own. But Don't Just Regurgitate Creative History, or Hold Art and Music and Literature as Fixed, Untouchable and Kept Under Glass. The People Who Try to "Guard" Any Particular Form of Music Are, Like the Copyists and Manufactured Bands, Doing It the Worst Disservice, Because the Only Thing That You Can Do to Music That Will Damage It Is Not Change It, Not Make It Your Own. Because Then It Dies, Then It's Over, Then It's Done, and the Boy Bands Have Won*

The thirteenth studio album by Chumbawumba (yes, the "Tubthumping" band) dedicates its entire title (and, like Soulwax, its cover art) to this 150+ word manifesto against the state of modern music and in favor of the English language.

Apparently, they are not big fans of pop music, which is a hard stance to take considering they created one of the biggest pop hits of the last few decades, but maybe they learned something from the experience. They did re-form themselves as an acoustic folk band when people weren't looking, after all. That's probably something you do when you get older and wiser.

The title tends to be shortened to *The Boy Bands Have Won . . .* , which is a bit gloomier than the real title, but way, way easier to say. Speaking of easier, the band's follow-up (and final) album was the dead-simple *ABCDEFG*. Maybe they thought they'd take it easy on us for their last hurrah. We're thankful for it.

The Seven
Longest Messages
Sent Into Space

If we are alone in the universe, truly alone . . . then we've got a lot of work to do to get all the stars arranged to say, "Kilroy was here." What else are we going to do with all of that crap up there?

But just in case we're not, we've collectively decided that every once in a while, we need to take the time to shout, "Hello? Is anybody there? Helloooo! We've invented pie! Come have a slice!" So far, we haven't had any takers, but if pie technology begins to ramp up the way these silly "computer" things have, it shouldn't be too much longer.

Of course, we're always spitting out random garbage into space. Radio and TV signals, mostly. But the signals on this list are intended specifically to attract aliens and get them to think we're cool and come hang out with us, and maybe ask us to prom.

7. The Entirety of *The Day the Earth Stood Still* (2008), 6,387 words

Hey, you know what aliens probably love? Movies that show what racist, xenophobic assholes we are as a species! That's sure to reel them in, right? Apparently, 20th Century Fox didn't really consider the content of the 2008 remake of *The Day the Earth Stood Still* before beaming it to Alpha Centauri, a star system only four light years away.

Since it was sent out in December 2008, that means that by the time you're reading this, any aliens near Alpha Centauri who were actually interested in watching it (judging by Earth numbers, that's a decent few) should have seen it. Thus, they'll have learned that we're complete idiots who are trashing our planet, but that we're also progressive enough to allow humanoid robots like Keanu Reeves star in feature films.

The movie itself is a bit shy of two hours long, and according to the script it's almost 6,500 words of dialogue (man, movies are short). Is that enough on which to judge our civilization? We may find out in about four years, if anybody replies. (That's assuming they're not just waiting for the movie to come out on video before watching it.)

6. The Voyager Golden Records,
??? words (about 2 hours)

In 1977, we launched the twin Voyager unmanned spacecrafts with the goal of seeking out new life and new civilizations. (Okay, not really, we just put them out there to collect data on gas giants and eventually take a gander at the universe outside our little solar system.)

Also included on both, though, are golden records and handy phonographs on which to play them, just in case any aliens happen to scoop them up. The records were designed by a committee led by über-awesome celebrity astronomer Carl Sagan. So hey, there's a chance that the first contact aliens have with our culture will have been created by one of the coolest humans we've ever had. Score one for us.

The records contain about five minutes' worth of "earth sounds" (think of those relaxation tapes, like ocean waves and whale songs), ninety minutes of music from all over the world, greetings in fifty-five different languages, and sixty minutes of Carl Sagan's girlfriend's brain waves, for some reason, making the whole thing about two hours overall.

Also, there are about 100 images, personalized messages from Earth dignitaries, and some pictographs drawn on the record covers. Yeah, it's a bit weird and kind of a hodge-podge of stuff, but it's not like we know what aliens are going to like and respond to. If they were anything like us, all we'd need to send is a bottle of vodka and a robot to give them a firm handshake and we'd be done.

5. ■ **A Commercial for Doritos,** 11,520 words

Okay, it turns out there's something way worse to send into space than a cheesy and potentially off-putting blockbuster movie, and that's the same Doritos commercial, over and over, for six hours. We can barely stand two minutes of commercials here on Earth. Six hours is considered a war crime under international law. Okay, well, it should be anyway. The ad was broadcast in 2008 and sent forty-two light years away to a star system called 47 Ursae Majoris, part of the Big Dipper. So, with luck, you've still got several decades of safety before this madness reaches its destination.

We're not exactly sure why Doritos felt the need to repeat the ad 720 times, but they did. Once would have been sufficient to advertise corn chips to aliens who might not even know what corn is, much less chips. Ten times would have gotten the point across that we were doing this on purpose. Anything beyond that is asking for a swift and powerful invasion.

Since the ad doesn't feature any words (it's simply an animation portraying some Doritos sacrificing another to a jar of Doritos salsa), it's theoretically palatable to aliens, unlike Doritos themselves, which might be poisonous to some E.T. or another. Regardless, we've calculated that the few (printed) words that do appear in the commercial add up to about 11,520 words through the repetitions.

Unfortunately, all of those words have to do with either Doritos or the retail transactions that would allow one to procure Doritos. That means that aliens' first experiences with human language may be solely related to the exchange of currency for junk food. So they're going to end up thinking the majority of our motivation as a species is to spend our resources on ephemeral, fleeting garbage. Well, it's not entirely off the mark, we guess.

4. 501 Social Media Messages,
25,000 words (approximate)

2008 was apparently a red-letter year for shouting into the cosmos. In addition to Fox and Doritos, social network Bebo decided to try their hand at contacting aliens with their "A Message from Earth" program.

Although hundreds of thousands of messages were submitted, the final selections were made by user votes (which were probably for whatever was popular in 2008) and staff picks. In the end, 501 messages, including some by celebrities and politicians, were beamed out toward Gliese 581 c, an extrasolar planet 119 trillion miles (a little over twenty light years) away.

The transmission took approximately four and a half hours. Users were also allowed to submit drawings and pictures instead of text, so there's no way of knowing exactly how many words we spat out into the heavens, but if we go with an average of fifty per message (a number we totally pulled out of our butts), then it's about 25,000 words. We may be wrong, and if we are, you're totally free to buy some scissors and glue and reorganize this list to reflect that.

3. 5,000 Messages from Across the Internet,
40,000 words (approximate)

For Penguin UK's 2010 release of *The Eerie Silence: Are We Alone in the Universe?* they solicited dozens of space-oriented websites to ask their users to come up with 5,000 messages to send into space, calling the promotion "Break the Eerie Silence." That's smarter than what we would have done, which would have been to build a Death Star–sized speaker just to play an enormous fart noise. We would have called it "Awkwardly Break the Eerie Silence."

Anyway, the 5,000 messages, which were chock full of corny "please pick me up" and MySpace-style jokes were sent out toward the Orion Nebula, about 1,350 light years away.

Since the texts were limited to forty characters, we can easily determine that around 40,000 words were sent, and, thankfully, we'll be long dead (probably of shame) before any aliens read them.

2. 25,800 Texts from Australians,
828,000 words (approximate)

Inspired by Bebo's "A Message from Earth" campaign, *COSMOS* magazine and the Australian government partnered up, Lethal Weapon style, in 2009 to create the cleverly titled "Hello from Earth," a repository of text messages that would be transmitted by NASA to Gliese 581 d (Gliese 581 c's big brother). (No, it's not a rip-off of Bebo's thing. It was *inspired by it*, okay?)

One thing they did differently from Bebo was they didn't bother filtering out the messages. Anything and everything that was sent to HelloFromEarth. net was packaged up and sent out, which ended up being 25,878 messages. Well, they didn't take *everything*. They did have moderators to make sure no one just submitted stuff like "haha poop" or whatever (which is why we didn't even bother submitting).

Since the messages were SMS length (160 characters) and we know there were 25,878 of them, we can average that out to five characters per word (which is the standard for casual writing) and arrive at about 828,000 words. Unfortunately, it's probably a whole mess of gobbledygook that aliens won't understand a lick of. We'll find out in forty years (Gliese 581 c and d are both approximately twenty light years away), we suppose.

1. 100,000 Craigslist Ads,
10,000,000 words (approximate)

In 2005, one of the most important messages in human history was beamed into space. "Free kittens to a good home." Aliens probably love kittens, don't you think? That's what Craigslist CEO Jim Buckmaster was betting on, anyway, when the company started a campaign to send posts into outer space.

All that was required of users was to check a box during posting and their ad for an old stinky couch, rusted lawnmower, or sexual proposition (they still had that board back then) was copied and beamed out to the stars. Why? Because why not? Aliens need to experience scams and idiots, too.

The ads, over 100,000 in all, were sent out by a commercial enterprise called Deep Space Communications Network. We figure an average of 100 words per post, which means that over 10,000,000 words worth of complete junk was sent to the cosmos. Have you ever been on Craigslist? Between the badly spelled ads and the insane things people actually try to sell, there's really no end to the weirdness that goes on there. If Craigslist were a real place, it could only be described as "oddly sticky."

Even if there were aliens in the market for a disturbingly stained used futon, the ads weren't sent to any place in particular, but an empty section of space about three light years away, which means we'd have already heard something by now. Or maybe, just maybe, we caught the ear of some hobo alien who's out of a job and he's slowly on his way here to see if that "secret shopper" job is still available.

The **Fifteen**
Longest
One-Syllable Words
in the English Language

Shorter words are great because, generally speaking, you're not going to confuse anyone with them. Of course, even short words can send you racing for a dictionary. But one-syllable words? No sir. Run. Stand. Cat. Dog. Some of our favorite words are one-syllable words (and our editors have asked us not to print them here, but if you use your imagination you'll probably think of a few).

But some short words hide in the dark recesses of the dictionary. The place where words stop being words and start turning into strange, hilarious, and fascinatingly mutated terms that shriek at the light of day. Oh, sure, you've seen some of these words before, but just wait until we get to their more bizarre brethren. Then you'll understand. Then you'll know what lurks beneath the pages on your bookshelf.

15. Screeched -v. (*skreecht*), 9 letters

WHAT IT MEANS: A harsh, shrill scream or cry. Birds screech, rodents screech, but most of all, damsels in Victorian-style gothic horror stories screech.

It can also mean to act like the goofy character Screech, played by Dustin Diamond in *Saved by the Bell*. (This is truly an awful fate—you may be doomed to fade into obscurity and end up the butt of a dictionary joke in our little book here.)

Also of note is the alternate, old-fashioned spelling of "scritched," which is nine letters long as well.

A SAMPLE SENTENCE: "She flung open the door and screeched in horror, as the mailman had delivered her new laptop and left it in the rain uncovered, slowly drowning the machine and turning its packaging into mush."

14. Scratched -v. (*skratcht*), 9 letters

WHAT IT MEANS: To break the surface of or otherwise blemish an object by scraping it with another rough or sharp object. You know, like when you get a brand new car and some jerk runs a shopping cart into it right away.

A SAMPLE SENTENCE: "He scratched off his last lottery ticket, expecting to be disappointed once again, but instead found a tiny message underneath that read, 'Help, they are keeping us captive in this lottery ticket printing factory, you are our only hope!'"

13. Scrounged -v. (*skrowngt*), 9 letters

WHAT IT MEANS: To attempt to gather resources by foraging. Squirrels and other little critters are fantastic at scrounging. Domestic ferrets also excel at this, usually by stealing the things you're looking for and hiding them until you rediscover them months later under the couch or behind the toilet.

Also applies to dumpster-diving hipsters looking to score free meals behind grocery stores, and those weird people on TV who never throw out anything—"just in case we might need it someday." Yep, you totally need all seventeen of those dead cats in your freezer, guy.

A SAMPLE SENTENCE: "I scrounged and saved for many months, and finally had the money to buy a new car, but the dealership only sold zeppelins, so that's why you now must refer to me as *Dreadlord Sky Captain Bonecruncher, Pilot of the Mighty Airship Skullshatterer.*"

12. **Scrunched** -v. (*skruncht*), 9 letters

WHAT IT MEANS: To compress or otherwise squeeze together. This happens when restaurants try to stuff your entire party of six into one booth, or what it's like for an average-sized adult to try to fit into an airline seat.

Scrunching is also a common sight at social events, where participants who don't want to be seen by other participants (either lame people they don't want to talk to or people they've specifically wronged) slump further and further into a chair in hopes that the person won't notice them. This never works.

(There's also the antiquated spelling of "scrinched," which is also a single syllable and nine letters long.)

A SAMPLE SENTENCE: "He scrunched up his face in concentration as he drew the string of the bow and prepared to fire the ruby arrow given to him by the dark wizard, who had sworn that its powers would allow him to immediately locate any taco stand within a fifteen-mile radius."

11. **Stretched** -v. (*strecht*), 9 letters

WHAT IT MEANS: To expand or draw out to the fullest extent. You know, get up and stretch your legs. Stretch your wallet to make the last few payments on that gorilla costume (you wouldn't think those things are expensive, but they totally are). Just think of Silly Putty.

Things can also be a metaphorical stretch, too. It's a stretch of the imagination to think we'll get a Pulitzer for this book, but we can dream. You'd have to stretch your imagination quite a lot to believe that politicians will ever tell the truth. (That's because it's genetically modified out of them by a secret government agency. Shh, don't tell anyone.)

A SAMPLE SENTENCE: "He stretched his arm as far as he could, but the key was just out of his reach; so it seemed he would die there, alone, with corn syrup dripping out of the tears in his flesh, and he wondered if anyone would remember the name *Stretch Armstrong* when he was gone."

10. Straights -n. (*strayts*), 9 letters

WHAT IT MEANS: Lengths without a bend, curve, or corner. Not to be confused with straits, which are small, thin connections between bodies of water, or Dire Straits, the band from the 1980s who made that video with the boxy people singing about how musicians didn't have to actually work for a living.

Straights can also be a slang term for people who are heterosexual, but you probably knew that if you've watched TV in the last thirty years or so. Point is, in that context, it's pretty easy to get a plural form of straight, whereas no one calls a grouping of straight lines "straights."

A SAMPLE SENTENCE: "When this horrible war started, it was brother against brother, as the letters of the alphabet chose sides based on their respective shapes, with *B, C, D, G, J, O, P*, and the rest forming the curves, and *A, E, F, H, I, K*, and their buddies making up the straights."

9. Strengths -n. (*strengths*), 9 letters

WHAT IT MEANS: To be mighty, like the bull. To be tough, like the walrus. To have emotional fortitude, unlike everyone in the theater during the first twenty minutes of the Pixar movie *Up*. You know, the first stat at the top of the Dungeons & Dragons character sheet. (The one you totally ignore if you're a badass frost wizard.)

Strengths, obviously, is the plural of that, like when you're taking an emotional inventory for your therapist and she asks what your strengths are, and you break down crying and admit that you once stole a dollar from the church collection plate.

A SAMPLE SENTENCE: "My many strengths include the ability to leap tall buildings in a single bound, go faster than a speeding bullet, shoot heat rays out of my eyes, freeze things with my breath, and fly around the world backward to turn back time, even though physics totally don't work that way."

8. Scraughed -v. (*skrawkt*), 9 letters

WHAT IT MEANS: Here we go, now we're getting into the weird stuff. Most of the following words, like scraughed here, are dialectical or just so old-fashioned that no one uses them anymore.

Scraughed, for example, is an old Scottish word meaning a loud, hoarse cry. So not a shrill cry like screeched, but more like a bellow. Obviously, this word came about because some poor drunken Scotsman walked off the side of a hill or something. There's really only so many ways you could describe what we're imagining that would sound like, anyway. We salute you, Scottish man that we just made up. You do good work around here.

A SAMPLE SENTENCE: "The elephant scraughed from deep inside his belly, but the lions, unsuspecting fools that they were, did not seem intimidated, and so the elephant narrowed his eyes and steeled himself for full-on combat."

7. **Sprainged** -v. (*sprayngt*), 9 letters

WHAT IT MEANS: To decorate something with colorful stripes. So, you know, every high school dance decoration ever made by some bored drama student, lots of varieties of women's clothes, and basically everything at a LGBT pride parade, because those folks have style.

Ever had a car that you put a racing stripe on? You just sprainged it. New tastefully striped wallpaper in your house? Totally sprainged. Fancy pin-stripe zoot suit? Sprainged like nobody's business.

A SAMPLE SENTENCE: "Jeb the Tiger had grown weary of his boring old black and orange stripes, so he went to a beauty store, bought all the hair dye he could find, and sprainged himself a very fashionable new coat."

6. **Throughed** -v. (*throod*), 9 letters

WHAT IT MEANS: To accomplish something or get something put through. Yeah, it's a weird one. You see, through was a verb once upon a time. If you did a rad presentation and everyone at work loved it, carried you out on their shoulders, and declared you the new CEO, you throughed it. It's an extremely old-fashioned form of the word.

Alternately, there's a super-old spelling of throw that's "throughe" and, theoretically you could say you throughed something against the wall, but even then, that was very uncommon. "Thrue" was the more likely spelling in that instance.

A SAMPLE SENTENCE: "Yeah, we went out for dinner, then saw a movie, then had some ice cream—and when we went home, her cat jumped on me and knocked me out the window . . . but I had totally throughed the date up until that point."

5. ■ Thrutched -v. (*thrucht*), 9 letters

WHAT IT MEANS: This is it, the end of the nine letter words. We hope you weren't too comfortable. Or maybe you were even getting . . . *fond* of them? It's okay, we understand. But, all things are fleeting, so we'll give you this one last hurrah with your nine-letter-loves.

Thrutched is a dialectical (that is, regional) term meaning to press, crush, or squeeze. So next time you grab breakfast someplace, make sure to ask for freshly thrutched orange juice and see how long it takes for them to decide if they need two or three people to throw you out.

It can also mean to be squeezed in a crowd, like if you accidentally stand in the mosh pit area before a Barry Manilow concert. (He has mosh pits, right? If not, he should.)

A SAMPLE SENTENCE: "I thrutched tightly around the tooth and began to pull, but he began to shout—it turns out that I didn't numb his mouth very well!"

4. ■ Schmaltzed -v. (*shmaltst*), 10 letters

WHAT IT MEANS: A Yiddish slang word that means false or exaggerated sentimentality. You've probably heard someone use it in old movies when they're trying to get on someone's good side. You know, "throw on a little schmaltz, they'll be all yours."

What it *actually* means is chicken grease. So what people are really saying is, essentially, greased up. Metaphorically speaking, that is. Please don't go to parties covered in chicken grease and expect anyone to be impressed by you.

A SAMPLE SENTENCE: "I went in, I schmaltzed a little, and before I knew it they were eating out of the palm of my hand." Literally.

3. Scraunched/Scrootched/Scroonched
■ -v. (*scrawncht, scroocht, scrooncht*), 10 letters

WHAT IT MEANS: We're making the bold decision to jam all these together because they're all just weird, depreciated spellings of pretty ordinary words. We'll go through them one by one.

Scraunched is a seventeenth-century form of crunched. It later became "scranched," dropping the *u* noise, then became "craunched," returning the *u* and dropping the *s*, and finally, "crunched," which actually didn't come into use until the 1800s.

Scrootched is a variation on "scrooched," which itself is a variation on "scrouched," a nineteenth-century word that eventually became "crouched." As it happens, a further variation, "scootched," is sometimes used in southern U.S. dialects today.

Finally, we have scroonched, which became "scrunched," which we talked about back at number twelve. We actually kept the *s* on the front of this one. Progress!

A SAMPLE SENTENCE: "I scraunched my way through the fallen leaves, then scrootched down when I saw the dark figure coming toward me, and fear led me to drop further back into the trees, where I scroonched down under a low limb—but as the figure got closer I realized it was just a run-of-the-mill wandering evil clown beast, and nothing to worry about at all."

2. Squirrelled -v. (*skwurlt*), 11 letters

WHAT IT MEANS: You probably have two objections to this one already. We understand. Firstly, no—that's not the standard way of spelling "squirreled."

It's an alternate spelling used primarily in England. Even a lot of them go with the one-*l* spelling these days, though.

Second, there's an ongoing debate on whether or not squirrelled actually has just one syllable or two, and the answer is: it depends. In many areas, squirrel is pronounced "skwer-el," but in many others, it can also be pronounced like "curl," which would make "squirrelled" sound something like "world," which is a single-syllable word. For what it's worth, the *Oxford English Dictionary*'s pronunciation has squirrel as a monosyllabic word. We could argue, but it's the freaking *OED*, man.

As for what the word actually means: To stash stuff away for future use. You knew that, though.

A SAMPLE SENTENCE: "I had squirrelled away my life savings and all the cash I earned in prison so that I could make a new life in the tropics, but on the final day before my release, I got into an argument with another inmate about whether squirrelled was one syllable or two, things got heated, he shivved me, and I had to spend all that money on hospital bills."

1. ■ Broughammed -v. (*brummed*), 11 letters

WHAT IT MEANS: You know how in movies set in the olden days, they'll sometimes have big, boxy carriages with a perch outside that the driver sits on? Like, every Dracula movie ever has one. That's a brougham (pronounced "brum"). You learned something new, right?

Well, broughammed means to arrive by or operate a brougham. Sort of like if you carted or trucked something, dig? So if you came to a fancy party by brougham, you could say that you were broughammed in. A homeless man carried by brougham through a bad part of town would be a bum broughhammed through a slum. (Okay, maybe that's a little much.)

A SAMPLE SENTENCE: "The driver broughammed us over the border, keeping his head down and speaking to no one, until finally we reached what we thought was the safety of the world's biggest ball of yarn, since none of us ever thought the kitten army would find us there—but oh, how wrong we were."

Schtroumpfed
-v. (*shtroompft*), 12 letters

WHAT IT MEANS: Consider this one a bonus, because it's actually a French word and not English (and it's a fictional word to boot), but we thought it was interesting all the same. In the original French, the Smurfs weren't the Smurfs. (The Smurfs were originally from a French-language Belgian comic book. Bet you didn't know that!) They were *Les Schtroumpfs*. So instead of going around smurfing everyone's smurf with their smurfing smurfs, they schtroumpfing schtroumpfed the schtroumpf out of some schtroumpf.

A SAMPLE SENTENCE: Schtroumpf you, man, we're all schtroumpfed out after that.

The **Thirty** Grossest Words in the English Language

Did you ever have an old uncle Leonard who would say horrible things to people, and now anytime you hear the word Leonard, you cringe a little? (Uncle Leonard has forever ruined *Star Trek* for us.) Well, these words are like that. They're words that immediately trigger the spot in your lizard brain that goes "blech."

So how does a fine book such as this one go about deciding something as subjective as grossness of words? Quite simply, we didn't. We did our own little informal survey on the Internet to find out which words people described as gross most often and ordered them by how common they appeared to be. Obviously, this is not scientific in the least, and we're sorry that our lab coats might have made you think that.

After that, we sat down and tried to explain why they're gross, then came up with innocuous sentences where an ordinary word is replaced with its gross synonym just to prove that context doesn't matter and these words are always nasty as hell.

One rule we set was that the words couldn't be sex terminology, juvenile slang, or complex medical jargon, because otherwise the list would be nothing but those. Coprophagia is gross (go look it up if you don't believe us), but it's not like it comes up in conversation that often. We set our sights on words that you might hear in daily use.

Oh, and if lunch is anywhere in your immediate past or future, come back to this section later.

30. ■ Fondle -v. *(fon-dul)*

WHY IT'S GROSS: Because fondling is never a good act. It only means bad things. You don't pick out oranges at the store by fondling them. You squeeze them, poke them, and check their skin for blemishes, which is gross-sounding enough, but even then, describing it as fondling goes way too far.

A SAMPLE SENTENCE: "He fondled his way through the dark, hands grasping this way and that, searching blindly for the light switch."

29. ▪ Slop -n. (*slop*)

WHY IT'S GROSS: Slop is what pigs eat. It's a big mix of mashed up corn and horse buttholes and who the hell knows what. You can call someone sloppy if they're not paying attention to what they're supposed to be doing, but you never tell anyone, "Hey, buddy, you remind me of a big ol' bucket of slop with your lack of attention to detail." That immediately goes from mild admonishment to weird and disgusting without even a pit stop.

A SAMPLE SENTENCE: "Dave sat down to his Thanksgiving dinner, beaming at his family and the large plate of slop before him, and he realized just at that moment that he'd never been so blessed."

28. ▪ Greasy -adj. (*gree-see*)

WHY IT'S GROSS: Because you're either talking about greasy food, which we already know is horrible for us thanks to years of news reports, or you're talking about greased-up flesh in some manner. Grease and the human body do not naturally coexist. Something has to put it there. It's not like you exercise for a few hours and get greasy with sweat. You get damp or even soaked, but greasy means, like, there's a film or something. A slick, oily one.

A SAMPLE SENTENCE: "I walked down the sidewalk and, while I wasn't paying attention, nearly slipped and fell in a big, greasy sheet of ice."

27. Crotch -n. (*krotch*)

WHY IT'S GROSS: The only things that tend to have crotches are us and trees, and tree crotches don't get all sweaty or have bodily waste near them. Basically, if you're looking for a neutral way to describe your genitals or the area they reside in, this isn't the word you're looking for. There are a whole lot of other words that don't sound like a storage place for unwanted things. "Oh, those boxes? Yeah, just stick 'em in my crotch and we'll sort through them later."

A SAMPLE SENTENCE: "Listen, I've brought you all together because the doctor just called and told me some shocking news, and I wanted you all to be the first to know about it, but we'll get through this together—plenty of people have been told they have crotch sickness and made it through just fine."

26. Bowel -n. (*bow-el*)

WHY IT'S GROSS: You ever had anything pleasant come out of your bowels? If so, thank you for reading this, Scarlett Johansson, but we all know that you are part of a superhuman species that has evolved beyond pooping.

There's nothing glamorous at all about bowels. Grosser still is "disembowel," which means you're taking that literal crap sack outside of someone's body for all of the rest of us to be repulsed and horrified by.

A SAMPLE SENTENCE: "He reached inside his bowels and felt around for his car keys, but grasped only empty air, and that's when he found the hole in his pants and realized the keys must have dropped out."

25. ■ Vomit -n., v. (*vom-it*)

WHY IT'S GROSS: We're not the only things that vomit, of course. Sometimes the Earth itself vomits forth a great blast of lava, for example. But we all know what imagery that term is meant to evoke, and that's stalking the porcelain dinosaur. Things vomit out in heaving sprays, like our dinner after a few too many Sprite Russians (that's a White Russian mixed with Sprite).

A SAMPLE SENTENCE: "He swished the mouthwash dutifully, just as his oral hygienist had showed him, leaned forward and vomited it all into the sink, then took a deep breath and thought how his mouth hadn't felt so clean in years."

24. ■ Viscous -adj. (*vis-kuss*)

WHY IT'S GROSS: There's only one viscous fluid in the world that's in any way pleasant, and that's pancake syrup. Anything else is toad slime or buffalo snot or something. If a liquid doesn't so much drip down as drop in clumps, it's probably not worth screwing with. There's a reason why aliens in movies always leave big, viscous hunks of creamy alien goo everywhere they go, and that is specifically to gross us out.

A SAMPLE SENTENCE: "The rain fell slowly at first, in big, viscous drops, but then it began to come down in sheets, and before I knew it, your mother and I were dancing and playing in it just like we were kids again."

23. ■ Squat -v. (*skwot*)

WHY IT'S GROSS: If you want to bring yourself low to the ground, you crouch or duck. You only squat if you're outside somewhere and about to go number two (or number one if you're a lady, or a man who just prefers going that way). (Hopefully you're outside, anyway. Or using one of those squat toilets, like they have in foreign countries sometimes.) Anyway, point is, squatting implies that you're about to do something gross. They call it "popping a squat" for a reason.

A SAMPLE SENTENCE: "He squatted down behind the bushes to take a closer look at the puddle of blood; the shocking realization that it was his blood overwhelmed him, and all of that relief was washed away."

22. Smear -v. (*smeer*)

WHY IT'S GROSS: Do you smear your jelly on your toast? Not unless it's KY Jelly, we're betting. No, smear is a term reserved for viscous or greasy things, so it's good that we already covered both of those words. Pigs smear mud on their bodies as they roll around in their pens. You don't smear out a blanket upon which to have a lovely picnic.

A SAMPLE SENTENCE: "A smile smeared across his face as he watched the children playing, and he realized how much he missed that innocence and naivety."

21. Feces -n. (*fee-sees*)

WHY IT'S GROSS: Crap, poop, dookie, even the *s*-word they won't let you say on TV (usually)—they all mean the same thing, and yet feces sounds grosser than any of them. We suspect because it's a clinical, medical term for the most disgusting part of our day. That contrast just really makes the difference. It's a clean word for a dirty act. "Defecate" takes a similar prize. If you break it down, it's literally "to remove the feces from yourself." Ew.

A SAMPLE SENTENCE: "He sighed heavily and shook his head at the sight before him, thinking to himself that every day it only got worse and worse, and soon enough he just wouldn't be able to deal with this feces anymore and might snap."

20. Rectum -n. (*reck-tum*)

WHY IT'S GROSS: Same reasons as previously mentioned. If you're mad at someone, you call them an asshole. If you call them a rectum, then an imaginary record needle scratches and everyone stops talking and stares. It's that clinical factor again, but also a little bit of bowel as well. Its close, personal friend "anus" has a similar gross factor. If anyone around you ever brings up their anus in casual conversation, then things have gone way too far.

A SAMPLE SENTENCE: "She was devastated when the press declared her new restaurant 'the rectum of the fine dining cuisine in the city,' so much so that she couldn't help dumping and unloading her displeasure on everyone she came across on that day."

19. Crusty -adj. (*krus-tee*)

WHY IT'S GROSS: As a word, "crust" is generally fine. Pizzas have crust. Pies have crust. Fried foods have an outer crust. No problem there. But crusty? No. Just no. If you describe your pie as crusty, you have done something terribly wrong. Untreated wounds are crusty. The Earth has the biggest crust around, but it's never crusty.

A SAMPLE SENTENCE: "Outside, I found my bed sheets hard and crusty from the night before, as Jim had apparently gotten drunk and tossed them out the window just before the ice storm hit."

18. Fester -n. (fess-tur)

WHY IT'S GROSS: Well, isn't it obvious? The only good fester is Uncle Fester, and even he's debatable. You, unfortunately, cannot stick a light bulb in a festering boil and have it adorably light up, even if your boil is extra-kooky and played by a heavily made-up Christopher Lloyd.

A SAMPLE SENTENCE: "It started as just an idea, but with time their idea to start an orphanage for the blind began to fester into something very unique and wonderful."

17. Discharge -n. (diss-charge)

WHY IT'S GROSS: Unless you're talking about being fired, no thanks. Discharged from the army? Fine. Discharged a firearm at the shooting range last weekend? Cool. Discharge from the cyst on your thigh? Gross. Discharge is generally not a big deal in its verb form, but in its noun form? You're not going to find many sympathetic ears, except maybe your doctor's.

A SAMPLE SENTENCE: "She squeezed and got nothing, so she tried harder a few more times until a thick, white discharge spewed out, and she thought to herself that she would have to remember to get a new bottle of shampoo next time she went to the store, because this one was nearly empty."

16. Backwash -n. (*back-wash*)

WHY IT'S GROSS: Backwash is like a sci-fi horror film. Some liquid went some place, but then *something from the other side came back with it.* Whether it's a sewer pipe that's backed up, or bits of chewing tobacco from your snuff-using friend that you foolishly let share your soda, it's the implication that something that was previously clean has been tainted by an outside source that makes backwash a word that basically has no benign uses.

A SAMPLE SENTENCE: "When the results came in, he let the backwash flow over him and realized that his campaign focus on cleaning up the sewer system had been a complete waste of time."

15. Curdle -v. (*cur-dull*)

WHY IT'S GROSS: You know what the expiration date on your milk is for, right? Those aren't flavor chunks. The word "curdle" brings to mind that smell you get when you thought you still had a day or two left on the last inch in that gallon jug. Now, technically, we get some good food from curdled milk, like cottage cheese and sour cream and stuff like that. We just don't really like to think about the fact that it got that way because it filled with bacteria that curdled it all into big, gross chunks of spoiled milk.

A SAMPLE SENTENCE: "Try our new beer formula, lovingly curdled in aged oak barrels for extra flavor."

14. Coagulate -v. (*co-ag-you-late*)

WHY IT'S GROSS: This is curdle's little brother. While it has the milk market cornered, "coagulate" holds court over blood and other thick substances.

Pudding, for example, can also coagulate, but for those kinds of things we usually use "congeal," itself a fairly gross word. Coagulate generally refers to your blood clotting up, usually outside of your body (though not always, if your blood has the consistency of Pepsi to begin with).

A SAMPLE SENTENCE: "He took out the frozen tube of coagulated orange juice, knowing that it was saving him money over buying it fresh, but still grumbling at the taste."

13. Excrete -v. (ex-creet)

WHY IT'S GROSS: Remember how we mentioned defecate earlier? Same story here. Excretion is not a pretty process at all. There's also "secrete," which isn't a whole lot better, but at least bees secrete honey and maple trees secrete sap for syrup, and those aren't terrible things. Excretion is generally a waste product, and not a delicious substance that we can use on pancakes.

A SAMPLE SENTENCE: "He knew he'd have to evacuate soon, and he grew more uncomfortable and shifted in his seat before finally reaching out to push the Excrete button on the control panel of his fighter jet."

12. Mucus -n. (myoo-cuss)

WHY IT'S GROSS: We're taught from a young age that boogers are disgusting and you should definitely not eat them or wipe them on the underside of your desk. Thus begins the long road to drilling it into human heads that anything that comes out of your nose is pretty damn gross. "Phlegm" falls under this same umbrella, for obvious reasons. Neither is a particularly good thing, doubly so when you consider that there are mucous membranes downstairs in the human body as well.

A SAMPLE SENTENCE: "He dragged himself underneath the old chassis, found the spot, and began twisting until the mucus poured out into the pan he'd laid on the ground underneath, wondering how much longer this banged-up car would last him."

11. Slobber -v. (*slob-er*)

WHY IT'S GROSS: You're only likely to encounter a few slobbering animals in your lifetime: big Cujo-esque dogs, really old cats, and humans who sleep with their mouth open. None of those are anything you want to screw with if you find an unknown one in your bed (we speak from experience). There's nothing enticing about someone sharing their spit with you, unless it's your first real date.

A SAMPLE SENTENCE: "The slow, constant slobber of the leaky faucet had been a mere nuisance at first, but at this late hour, the day before his big presentation, he thought it might slowly drive him insane."

10. Spurt -v. (*spurt*)

WHY IT'S GROSS: Spurt means the same thing as words like "spray" or "stream," but there's this added concept of forcefulness behind it. Lazy mountain streams don't tend to spurt. In fact, much of the time spurting has a biological connotation, like a spurt of blood or of . . . well, use your imagination. Squirt's in the same wheelhouse, but at least squirt guns are still fairly innocent. Not so much for our briefly produced "Spurt Guns." They made it a whole two days on store shelves!

A SAMPLE SENTENCE: "It spurted forth, hot and bubbling, and landed with a wet smack on the ground, rolling toward the village below that had been built in the volcano's shadow."

9. ■ Pus -n. (*puhss*)

WHY IT'S GROSS: If you ever had acne as a teenager (you did, don't lie), then you know exactly why pus is gross. If there were a list of the most appealing fluids on earth, natural spring water and fresh honey would be somewhere at the top, and pus would be putting up an awesome fight for dead last with garbage water, hobo spunk, and chunky vomit. You might be thinking, "Gosh, book, pus isn't all that terrible. I popped a lot of zits in my day." Sure, tiny amounts of pus might not be that awful, but we submit that you need only think of a styrofoam cup nearly filled to the brim with pus mysteriously appearing on your kitchen counter one morning to truly understand.

A SAMPLE SENTENCE: "The deep gash in its side had begun filling with pus, and I put my hand over it, feeling the stickiness seep between my fingers as I swore revenge on the loggers who had marked these trees."

8. ■ Seepage -n. (*seep-ige*)

WHY IT'S GROSS: Well, we just used the verb form in that last sample sentence, so you tell us. Seepage basically means a total lack of control, like leakage, but grosser sounding, especially in a biological context. You never, ever want anything on your body to be leaking or seeping. There's no positive way to have that happen. Even though "taking a leak" is pretty common to hear, it's still urinating, which isn't the most attractive thing in the world.

A SAMPLE SENTENCE: "After two days, the seepage hadn't stopped, and he'd begun to worry that he might really be in trouble this time, since his boat wasn't exactly in the best condition to begin with."

7. Orifice -n. (*or-if-iss*)

WHY IT'S GROSS: While an orifice can technically mean an opening on anything, we pretty much use it solely for holes in organisms, and none of those produce pleasant things. If our bodies were perfect machines, we wouldn't have waste products and thus, theoretically, wouldn't need orifices at all. No earwax, or boogers, or poo. What a grand life, indeed. Even the tiny little pores all over your body are orifices, with sweat as their waste. Really, when you look at how much waste we dump out through our orifices (no pun intended), is it any wonder that we leave a lot of trash behind?

A SAMPLE SENTENCE: "He looked through the orifice at the gray wetness, sighed, and thought how he really couldn't wait for this endless rainy season to finally be over and done."

6. Scrotum -n. (*skro-tum*)

WHY IT'S GROSS: Oh, that little bag of skin. Of all the sweaty parts of our bodies, scrotums get singled out as sounding the grossest. We can think of a couple of reasons. It's a bag that's (usually) covered in hair. It's right next to, and within farting distance of, the anus. It hangs out (literally) in a warm, enclosed space all day. (Please keep your scrotum in that enclosed space at all times while in public, fellas.) It's like a perfect storm of body horror miasma.

A SAMPLE SENTENCE: "She reached into the scrotum and quickly pulled out a handful of change."

 Menstruation -n. (*men-stroo-a-shun*)

WHY IT'S GROSS: The other side of the genital coin gets its grossness, too. Over the millennia, humans have developed an aversion to blood. Go figure. When that blood comes from sensitive places, our primate minds scream out, "*Warning! Danger! What is going on?*" We've learned to ignore it over time, but that doesn't mean that talking about it has improved much. Say "menstruation" ("menses" or "menstrual" works, too) in a crowded room and watch people of both sexes get a little grossed out.

A SAMPLE SENTENCE: He held a stained cloth against the menstruation, but the blood wouldn't stop—her wound was far too deep.

Splat -n. (*splat*)

WHY IT'S GROSS: Only the wettest, squishiest things make a splat noise when striking a hard surface. It's onomatopoeia intended specifically for that purpose. Nothing pleasant makes a splat noise when it falls, except for delicious cake, and even then it's kind of terrible because now you have to clean it up as well as missing out on eating it. Its grossness is directly related to the word "splatter," which is also highly unpleasant, especially when it involves a bathroom.

A SAMPLE SENTENCE: He heard the wet splat before he even knew it was coming and his stomach clenched at the sight of the pizza dough hitting the floor.

 Panties -n. (*pant-ees*)

WHY IT'S GROSS: Believe it or not, this word and the two that follow were rated as being the grossest words by more people than the rest of these combined.

Also of note is that "panties" was cited as a gross word almost exclusively by women. European women were especially opposed to it, much preferring the terms "pants" or "knickers," which are definitely more classy. Panties has an air of childishness about it that almost borders on pedophilic. It's especially creepy and gross coming out of the mouths of older men.

A SAMPLE SENTENCE: "The Marines issued them everything, from shirts to boots to panties, anything the men would need to make it through the next weeks of hell."

2. ■ **Ointment** -n. (*oint-ment*)

WHY IT'S GROSS: When's the last time you heard of someone using an ointment on something that *wasn't* disgusting? Probably never, right? It just doesn't happen. Ointments are for horrible things, like hemorrhoids and goiters and who knows what else. Also, they're almost inevitably greasy, slimy concoctions, like they're made out of pure jellyfish or something. The word immediately conjures up rashes and STD outbreaks. And no, calling it "cream" doesn't help, either.

A SAMPLE SENTENCE: "He smeared the ointment on himself thoroughly and deliberately, knowing that if he missed a spot, the pain would be just as bad as the last time he had gone to the beach without proper sun protection."

1. ■ **Moist** -adj. (*moyst*)

WHY IT'S GROSS: Far and away, this word is frequently said to be the absolute grossest. There's something about it that triggers the gross alarm in way too many people's heads for it to be a coincidence. If moist were a person, it would be that kid in your seventh-grade class who never showered. Let's look at some things that are moist: towelettes, the hands and underarms of a nervous guy at a party, the boxes in your pantry before you discovered the rat living there. Strangely, using the word "damp" instead doesn't seem to have the same effect. People are okay with damp things, but moist is apparently over the line.

A SAMPLE SENTENCE: "He made sure his mouth was nice and moist before he continued eating, because it had gone dry after all of those potato chips and he wanted to get to the rest of his dinner."

The **Thirty** Prettiest Words in the English Language

You made it through all of those gross words, so how about a palate cleanser? Let's look at the other side of the coin. These words just make you feel fancy when you say them. They're the linguistic form of a nice, refreshing shower. They roll off the tongue like a spring wind, and they also make you more attractive and rich. (Note: They do no such things.)

J. R. R. Tolkien once declared "cellar door" to be the most beautiful phrase in English. That's nice and all, but cellar doors are kind of creepy, don't you think? So we're aiming for words that are also semantically nice as well, because it would ruin it if a word like "cellador" (no one ever said we were original) meant "clogged douche nozzle" or "creepy kid who eats paste."

We'll also throw in a sample sentence, but just the opposite of those in the gross words list. These will be relatively disgusting sentences, but with nice and pleasant words added in. Unfortunately, change of context or not, they'll probably still turn out gross. Oh well!

30. Porcelain -n. (*por-seh-lin*)

WHY IT'S PRETTY: Yes, they make toilets out of it, but come on, there's other stuff made out of porcelain, too, like sinks and tiles. Still, it's a word that should, theoretically, evoke images of cleanliness and sanitation. *Theoretically.* Not only that, though; porcelain itself is strong enough to hold your butt, yet shatters easily if struck. It's that odd, counterintuitive mix of strength and fragility that gives it (and the word) a very poignant feel. Also, it sounds wicked badass when it breaks. It's like glass, but approximately three times more awesome.

A SAMPLE SENTENCE: "The shards of porcelain stuck in his face and neck; he tried to stand, but the combination of the loss of blood and the weight of the fallen china hutch made it practically impossible."

29. ■ Diffuse -v., adj. (*diff-yoos*)

WHY IT'S PRETTY: In its verb form, diffuse means to spread or scatter, and usually refers to things like liquid or light—stuff that you can actually scatter, you know. Crop dusters, for example, diffuse their payload over a wide area. But as an adjective, diffuse also has the implication of these things being evenly spread out. In the first *Indiana Jones* they used that cool staff to take the diffuse light and concentrate it into a single beam. You get what we're saying? If something is diffuse, it kind of has that feel of controlled chaos . . . unlike that fourth *Indiana Jones* movie.

A SAMPLE SENTENCE: "He admired the results of his hard work, entrepreneurship, and forethought, as he had managed a very diffuse distribution of the pornography among the crowds."

28. ■ Aesthetic -adj. (*es-thet-ick*)

WHY IT'S PRETTY: Well, come on, the word itself means to have pleasing, beautiful attributes. Isn't it convenient that they gave the word itself an aurally pleasing sound? A little too convenient, if you ask us. Still, it's the most straightforward pretty word you can get, because it's meta as hell.

A SAMPLE SENTENCE: "He smiled at the aesthetic perfection of the collection of severed heads, delicately stacked like a supermarket soup can display."

27. ■ Domicile -n. (*dome-iss-ile*)

WHY IT'S PRETTY: It means home, although not in that warm, fuzzy kind of way that the word "home" itself conjures up. A cardboard box could be a domicile, but it's not likely to be a home (more likely it's "the place where I pass out after my meth high wears off"). Still, it's just a nice sounding word, like "dinosaur," but hopefully with more tasteful area rugs and coffee tables. What's more likely to resonate with the ladies? "Step into my murder chamber," or "please, enter my domicile"? (Yes, those are your only two choices.)

A SAMPLE SENTENCE: "We looked at the massive piles of discarded food wrappers, holding our noses as she said, 'This is my domicile, and I'd appreciate it if you wiped your feet before you came in.'"

26. Evocate -v. (ev-oh-kate)

WHY IT'S PRETTY: It's always nice to see a word that can be easily broken down into its base parts. Evocate, for example, has *voc*, as in voice, right in the middle, with *e* (the Latin prefix for the preposition "out") at the beginning, so with about three seconds of thought you can put together that it means to call out or summon. Also, it sounds like a term wizards use, like evoking the spirits to get them to take out their wizard trash and stuff.

A SAMPLE SENTENCE: "As he held the prostitute's lifeless body in his arms, he began to evocate over and over, 'Mother, I've done it again!'"

25. Cathedral -n. (cath-ee-dral)

WHY IT'S PRETTY: Look, even if you're not religious, you have to admit that a big, beautiful Gothic cathedral is an awesome sight. Come on, they've got gargoyles. You can't put gargoyles on anything else (except maybe old buildings like the one in *Ghostbusters*) without it looking totally ridiculous.

And then there's the stained glass! You could put together a mosaic of early '90s fashion out of stained glass and it would still look amazing and classy.

A SAMPLE SENTENCE: The beauty of the cathedral awed everyone in the tour group, but the odor left a lot to be desired.

24. Efflorescence -n. (*eff-lor-ess-ens*)

WHY IT'S PRETTY: Efflorescence means the state of flowering. Don't tell us you're not into flowers. Even the manliest bro (broliest bro?) can dig the smell of spring in bloom. Unless you have hay fever or something, we guess. Still, it sounds bright and colorful and fancy. It's pretty much untouchably pure and beautiful. Darth Vader could say it over a death metal guitar solo and it'd still be considered the most uplifting song of the year.

A SAMPLE SENTENCE: "The flowers began their bright red efflorescence, triggering a sneezing fit, and she knew that walking down this winding road had been a terrible mistake."

23. Luxurious -adj. (*lucks-your-ee-us*)

WHY IT'S PRETTY: Well, who doesn't like luxury? Whether your idea of luxury is a private jet with a runway right outside your house, John Travolta-style, or just a week off work and a big stack of books, there's no way anyone can argue with you about it. It's whatever you already love, times 23.96 percent (this is an actual mathematical formula that we just made up). The act of buying something more luxurious than what you already have feels nice, even if you had to put it on your last non-maxed credit card. Also luxurious?

Long-haired cats. Just ask that bald James Bond villain with the big, white kitty. Pet one today!

A SAMPLE SENTENCE: "Well, Your Honor, I loved the luxurious way the inside of that fur coat felt, so I thought I would make fresh ones to share that feeling with everyone in my family."

22. Amorous -adj. (*am-or-us*)

WHY IT'S PRETTY: Because it means dealing with love, d'aww! Even if you're one of those ratty old curmudgeons who doesn't believe in love, you can still be amorous for other things, like dolphins. (Just kidding, it only means romantic/sexual love, and we assume you wouldn't screw a dolphin.)

A SAMPLE SENTENCE: "He felt amorous toward her the moment he saw her through the restaurant window, so he immediately ran inside and robbed her with a gleam of love in his eyes."

21. Transcendent -adv. (*tran-send-ent*)

WHY IT'S PRETTY: Transcendent means to be able to rise above something, like adversity or the annoying chatter of your coworkers with a well-timed push of the Close Doors button on the elevator. (Despite what you may have read on the Internet, those do sometimes still work.) Transcendental meditation, for example, was all the rage for a couple of years because all you have to do is quit thinking of all the crap that bugs you and put yourself above it. Sounds nice, doesn't it? (Note that it does not work against debt collectors. We tried.)

A SAMPLE SENTENCE: "As he looked out over all the little ant-like people below, he felt transcendent and carefree, smiling to himself as he spat one wad of gum off the roof after another."

20. Smirk -n. (*smurk*)

WHY IT'S PRETTY: Smiles are cool. We're not down on smiles or anything. But smirks? Way, way better, in that mysterious kind of way. You catch the attention of that guy or lady you like and he or she is kind of disinterested—then you nail 'em with the joke about the family trying out for the variety show. Maybe he'll put on a little smirk, maybe she'll avoid eye contact and mutter under her breath. Sometimes we have trouble telling which way that situation will lead.

A SAMPLE SENTENCE: "She smirked at him as he tried to stand up, as she had already taken care of that possibility with a few well-placed nails in his ankles."

19. Melody -n. (*mell-oh-dee*)

WHY IT'S PRETTY: Come on, this one isn't hard. Melodies are one of the reasons we like music. (Unless you listen to weird, experimental music, anyway. If you do, be sure to corner people you hate at parties and talk to them about it for an hour or two.) It's an added bonus that the word melody itself sounds, well, rather melodious. At this point in human development, it's probably one of the top five things of which we should be pretty proud.

A SAMPLE SENTENCE: "He loved the sounds of the giant tree-shredding machine, and he especially enjoyed the way the melody and timbre changed when he inserted a whole Christmas tree, stolen from his neighbor's house, into the main loader."

18. Velvet -n. (*vell-vet*)

WHY IT'S PRETTY: Much like melody, velvet just sounds . . . velvety. It's soft and kind of fuzzy, like a baby's head, except that you don't have to worry so much about dropping it that you freak out and start screaming the second someone hands it to you. It's smooth, like velvety jazz, and delicious, like red velvet cupcakes. Nothing terrible has ever been described as velvety. There's no "Velvet Killer" who strangles his victims with fancy fabric. (Not until we finish our debut crime novel, anyway.)

A SAMPLE SENTENCE: "The inside of the outfit felt like warm velvet against his skin, and he knew he'd finally found the gimp suit he had been looking for all these years."

17. Petrichor -n. (*pet-re-kor*)

WHY IT'S PRETTY: Chances are you don't know this one, so here goes: You know that nice, earthy smell the ground gets after a fresh rain? That's petrichor. Now, we'll be the first ones to admit that the word itself isn't exactly gorgeous. It has "ichor" right there at the end. In fact, it's probably the ugly duckling of this list. But that smell? Oh man, if they made that as a car air freshener . . . well, we're not legally allowed to own vehicles after our impromptu demolition derby at the elementary school playground. But it'd still smell *great.*

A SAMPLE SENTENCE: "With the smell of petrichor fresh in his nose, he walked through the still-damp woods and whistled, switching the sack full of stolen mailboxes from one shoulder to another."

16. Epiphany -n. (*ee-piff-a-nee*)

WHY IT'S PRETTY: We just had a thought. What if there was a word that described that moment where the perfect idea comes to you, right when you need it, and if you're in a movie or on a TV show triumphant music plays and the plot can finally go forward? We'd call it something beautiful, like Hasselhoff. (Our editors just told us that word already exists. We know, it means "an actor everyone pretends to like for laughs." Hah, too easy.)

A SAMPLE SENTENCE: "He had a sudden epiphany that solved his 'streaking is illegal in most countries' problem once and for all."

15. Lithe -adj. (*lythe*)

WHY IT'S PRETTY: It means supple or pliant, like a ballerina or a really tall weed from that year you didn't bother mowing your grass all summer. It's one of those words that sounds exactly like what it means. It's dextrous and stretchy, like a team of gymnasts got in a fight with a Silly Putty tentacle monster in a bouncy castle.

A SAMPLE SENTENCE: "Her lithe frame allowed her to fit into very tight spots, which meant that it was no problem to stuff herself into the train's storage compartment and attack her target when the time was right."

14. Mellifluous -adj. (*mell-if-loo-us*)

WHY IT'S PRETTY: Okay, it's a bit of a tongue twister, we'll admit. Still, mellifluous has a very relevant meaning here: It's used to describe something as sweet-sounding. In fact, if you break the word down into its Latin roots, it's even more literal than you'd imagine. *Melli* (or *mel*) means honey, and *flu* (as in fluid) means flow. So it really does mean sweet-sounding, as in it sounds like honey. Interesting fact: The antonym of mellifluous is "Tom Waits."

A SAMPLE SENTENCE: "The sound of the garbage man's distress at the smell of my trashcan was quite mellifluous to my ears."

13. Cerebral -adj. (*sir-eeb-rul*)

WHY IT'S PRETTY: Hey, who doesn't like a brainy person? It's fancy-sounding enough that Professor X named his computer Cerebro. Then again, he also named his school "Charles Xavier's School for Gifted Youngsters." Brevity is the soul of wit, Charles. (Also, who says "youngsters" anymore?)

A SAMPLE SENTENCE: "The murderer's cerebral wit had allowed him to get away with his crimes so far, but now we had firm evidence, in the form of a Facebook picture that he accidentally made public, that could put him away forever."

12. Gossamer -adj. (*goss-a-mur*)

WHY IT'S PRETTY: James "Rotgut" McStevens once said, "There's nothing quite as pretty as a cobweb covered in dew on a spring morning, except maybe a cow with her head stuck in the fence." It's disturbing, but it certainly makes you think, mostly about how we just made all of that up! Gossamer objects include spider webs, silk veils, and anything made of fine, delicate string. Basically, anything that would get destroyed if you looked at it funny. It's pretty for the same reason babies are cute—because it's hilarious when they throw up on people. Wait, no, it's their fragility and innocence.

A SAMPLE SENTENCE: "The gossamer threads that held her robe together were made specifically to fall apart 'by accident' at the slightest touch."

11. Halcyon -adj. (*hal-see-on*)

WHY IT'S PRETTY: For one thing, it sounds like a ship from some crazy space opera. Ten bucks says there was a ship in *The Matrix* trilogy called *Halcyon* at some point. What it actually means is tranquil, peaceful, worry-free. The halcyon days of old, where you sat on the porch on a cool afternoon in late summer, sipping a beer with your neighbor while the kids played ball down at the old dirt field. (You are free to substitute your particular cultural fantasy of choice, of course.)

A SAMPLE SENTENCE: "In those halcyon days, he could go six, maybe seven hours without writing letters of angst to his ex-girlfriend, but these days, if he stopped doing it at all, he felt like he was letting himself down."

10. Serenity -n. (*sir-en-it-tee*)

WHY IT'S PRETTY: Like halcyon, serenity is a state of calm peacefulness. Unlike halcyon, it's much easier to spell. Regardless, serenity tends to be more of a personal term than halcyon. An unflappable, older priest confronting a demon-possessed child is serene, for example. Serenity is also a cheap excuse for nerds to make *Firefly* jokes, something we've had to restrain ourselves from doing.

A SAMPLE SENTENCE: "She couldn't help but feel the serenity in the air moments before the crowd burst into applause and she stepped into the Jell-O wrestling pit."

9. ■ Bungalow -n. (*bung-a-lo*)

WHY IT'S PRETTY: We'll be the first ones to point out that this word has "bung" in it, so let's all take a moment and reflect on that. Finished? Okay. There are a lot of words for small living spaces—apartment, dorm, flat, and so on—but none of those are nearly as fun to say as bungalow. It sounds like the kind of place you'd want to live in as a kid, like it's got a trampoline stashed in one of the bedrooms or something.

A SAMPLE SENTENCE: "Inside his bungalow, a series of old-fashioned freezers were lined up against one wall, and in each one, he'd stashed a single body part in hopes of one day constructing a real-life snowman."

8. ■ Dulcet -adj. (*dull-set*)

WHY IT'S PRETTY: Hey, it means pleasant to the ear, and that's what we're doing here. It usually refers specifically to music, i.e., "the dulcet tones of Uncle Steve's badly-out-of-tune accordion," but you get the idea. It's like mellifluous, but more folksy and charming, or maybe that's just because it makes us think of dulcimers, and that gets us thinking about dear old Uncle Steve again. May he (and that accordion) rest in peace.

A SAMPLE SENTENCE: "The dulcet sounds of the orchestra could only do so much to muffle the hellish wail of the amateur bagpipe recital a mile away."

7. ■ Capricious -adj. (*cap-ree-shee-us*)

WHY IT'S PRETTY: To be capricious is to be whimsical and quick to change one's mind, or in modern parlance, adorkable, or whatever we're supposed to be calling it these days. So think of Zooey Deschanel and you've got capricious. Basically, it's an old-fashioned word for the manic pixie dream girl, except it isn't gender specific. Breaking it down even further, it's essentially just a really fanciful term for severe Attention Deficit Disorder.

A SAMPLE SENTENCE: "Her capricious nature meant that she was always picking out her next victim before the previous one had even begun to smell funny."

6. ■ Surreptitious -adj. (*sir-up-tish-us*)

WHY IT'S PRETTY: For one thing, it sounds like syrup, and you can never go wrong there, especially if it's cough syrup that you don't have a prescription for. But surreptitious means stealthy or sneaky. Not in a ninja sense; more in a political fashion, usually. Think of Tom Cruise in *Valkyrie* (where he played the Nazi who tried to kill Hitler) as opposed to Tom Cruise in *Mission: Impossible*. Technically, it's not a purely positive word, but it's awesome that it sounds as sneaky as its meaning.

A SAMPLE SENTENCE: "I was surreptitious as I went about slowly stacking the chicken bones outside Matt Damon's house, because I knew that if anyone saw me, I wouldn't be able to complete the ritual to end the world."

5. Crisp -adj. (*krisp*)

WHY IT'S PRETTY: From the crisp sound of walking on fallen leaves or fresh snow to a crisp wind in the spring, you're pretty much covered with crisp year round. And no, we don't mean the English word for chips. (The fact that we are actually covered in Dorito crumbs is of no consequence here.) Crisp has an onomatopoeia to it, too, like the sound of someone biting into a fresh apple (but before the part where they find the razor blade some psychopaths who are not us stuck inside).

A SAMPLE SENTENCE: "The knife made a crisp, purring sound as it cut through the tent and exposed the unexpecting stoned teenagers inside."

4. Opulent -adj. (*opp-you-lent*)

WHY IT'S PRETTY: Well, opulent means rich, like an opulent palace, but let's not get snooty and elitist about this. We can all be equally jealous of the rich *together*. The human spirit of community is in bad-mouthing people who have it better than we do. That's just common sense. Anyway, opulent also sounds like opal, which is either a beautiful gem or your obnoxious grand-mother, depending on your life experience.

A SAMPLE SENTENCE: "He loved hearing the opulent and wealthy cry, complain, and beg when he held them upside down over a smelting pot operating at max temperature."

3. Leisure -n. (*lee-zure* or *lez-yoor*)

WHY IT'S PRETTY: Everyone likes being at leisure, except the British, because they prefer to be at leisure. That's just a little language joke, and we're not very proud of it because it may not come across very well in print, but we're soulless husks. They probably use jokes like that to calibrate torture devices. Anyway, however you pronounce it, leisure is just a relaxing word, both for the connotations and for the way you just slur the *s*, like you stopped giving a crap about halfway through.

A SAMPLE SENTENCE: "'True leisure,' he said as he began walking into the alligator pit, 'is something that everyone needs, but for which few are willing to pay the price.'"

2. **Turquoise** -adj. (*tur-kwoys*)

WHY IT'S PRETTY: In addition to the lovely blue-green hue of the actual gem, turquoise is just a pleasant word to say aloud. Go on, try it. Do it again. Keep saying it, over and over, while we use our echolocation system to find you and steal your wallet.

A SAMPLE SENTENCE: "The turquoise color of his shirt became muted by the color of the ocean as he sank to the bottom, feet encased in cinder blocks."

1. **Mother** -n. (*muh-ther*)

WHY IT'S PRETTY: Because about 40,000 people say so. According to an *actual* survey conducted by the British Council among English speakers, mother is the most beautiful word. We can dig it. The very concept of motherhood has been a tremendous influence on human development. Just look at the *Alien* franchise, for example. That Alien Queen? Totally the ideal mother.

A SAMPLE SENTENCE: "The mother in her wanted to hold him and comfort him, but that had gone terribly wrong the last dozen times she had tried it."

The Four Greatest Historical Contributors to the English Language

Let's invent a word. Right now. It's going to mean, uh . . . "to create a word on the spur of a moment." That word is going to be, er . . . scibuto! Right, so, scibuto. How do we get people to start using this word? We could try sliding it into everyday conversation. "Last night, I stayed up all night scibuting because the dictionary just wasn't doing it for me anymore." Maybe you fine people reading this book will pick it up and start using it every day. That'll help. We'll be in the *Oxford English Dictionary* in no time flat!

Or we could write some of the most influential works in the history of the language and, indeed, literature as a whole, and use our vast intellects to combine, construct, refine, and borrow words into new, unrecognizable shapes. That's what the following four writers did, and now dozens of words they invented are part of our lexicon as a result. (That's all way too much work for us, but we're still holding out hope for you, scibuto.)

4. William Shakespeare: 1560(?)–1616

Bet you weren't expecting this guy to come in last place, were you? Despite his fame for coming up with thousands of words for his plays, modern estimates have found that the real number is probably much lower, with some experts saying it may actually be as low as 200. (He really *did* invent hundreds of popular phrases that we still use, however, like "all's well that ends well" and "faint-hearted," so don't write Bill off completely.) Shakespeare actually has some really stiff competition, as you'll see.

Writing on the cusp of the movement from Middle English to Modern English, Shakespeare and his fellows on this list were pretty much our last hurrahs at inventing a bunch of new words before the language settled down into what it's been for nearly the last 500 years.

Shakespeare was particularly notorious for taking existing words from English, French, or Latin and utilizing them as different parts of speech than usual. For example, he took "amaze" and turned it into "amazement," "fashion" became "fashionable," and "sanctimony" became "sanctimonious." Whether or not you consider those to actually be new words is between you and a whole bunch of scholars who do nothing but argue about it. They don't even eat or breathe or poop. They just argue.

SOME WORDS ATTRIBUTED TO HIM: Eyeball, puking, assassination, dishearten, lackluster, outbreak, unreal, gloomy, moonbeam, scrubbed

3. John Donne: 1572–1631

A contemporary of old Willy Shakespeare, John Donne's contributions to the arts were in the form of poems instead of plays, which also gave him ample opportunity to tool around with wordplay and language.

You may not know Donne's name, but we bet you've heard some of his famous quotations, such as "no man is an island," and "ask not for whom the bell tolls." (Fun fact: He also filled in on the drums for Lars Ulrich during the recording of the *Metallica* song "For Whom the Bell Tolls" at the ripe old age of 413.)

Like Shakespeare, Donne also borrowed and modified existing words, but a lot more of his seem to be genuinely original instead of just being the first popular use of existing words (like how most everyone knew "show me the money" before *Jerry Maguire*, but that was what turned it into a huge deal). It's estimated that he gave us somewhere around 300 new words.

Keep in mind that Shakespeare had little formal education. He just had a crapload of work published, and thus a crapload of words credited to his name. Donne, on the other hand, was exceptionally well educated, which is probably why his smaller pool of published works still contains more new words than Shakespeare's.

SOME WORDS ATTRIBUTED TO HIM: Bystander, reunion, derelict, becalming, nonconformity, aberration, clinic, emergency, inconceivable, perplexing

2. Ben Jonson: 1572–1637

A fellow playwright during Shakespeare's time, Ben Jonson has not been nearly so famous, but still contributed a whole lot of words—somewhere around 550—to the English language. Unlike Shakespeare, he stuck primarily to comedies, however, when his tragedies turned out to be unsuccessful.

As it happens, he, too, was a well-educated poet like Donne, but he hasn't been as popular in that regard, either. So the moral of that story is to do one thing extremely well instead of two things extremely well. Wait, that's a terrible moral. In Jonson's case, it's true, though. While he was technically adept at both things and probably would have been very successful in any other period in history, he just got totally outshone by his various contemporaries of the time. (In modern times, that is. In his heyday, he was totally a big deal and probably got lots of fly honeys.)

SOME WORDS ATTRIBUTED TO HIM: Masterpiece, bookworm, conscious, exotic, graphic, essayist, parody, magnetic, guitar, antiquated

1. ■ John Milton: 1608–1674

John Milton, the author of the greatest piece of fanfic of all time, *Paradise Lost*, not only contributed tons of new stuff to Christianity (about 70 percent of what you think is in the Bible actually came from *Paradise Lost*, we guarantee you), but also brought us more than 600 new words. Not who you expected to see in first place, is it? (We thought for sure it would be Snoop Dogg, but adding -izzle to something apparently doesn't make it a new word, according to *some* philistines.)

It's worth noting that Milton was significantly younger than the other gentlemen on this list, as all of them (except Jonson, who died five years later) were dead by the time Milton even finished school. So he already had all of their contributions to work with, and *still outdid all of them.*

Oh, and did we mention that by the time he was working on his most important stuff (*Paradise Lost* included), he was *totally blind*? He dictated all of his work to assistants who transcribed his speech. Now, as far as handicaps go, no, you technically don't need sight to write (or to read. Hi, blind folks!), but it certainly doesn't make it any easier. Or maybe it does. Just to be on the safe side, we all blinded ourselves a while back and began dictating this book to impoverished immigrant children with a middling understanding of English. Let us know how it's going!

WORDS ATTRIBUTED TO HIM: Debauchery, terrific, lovelorn, stunning, apocalyptic, criticize, ecstatic, framework, ammunition, created (yes, *he created the word* "created")

How a **Meme** Became the Most Popular Word in the Whole World

It's commonly said that an enormous number of children from all over the world can recognize Mickey Mouse before they can recognize a U.S. President. (To be fair, seriously, what have the presidents done for kids versus what Mickey Mouse has done for them? Also, there's a bunch of those guys we don't even recognize. Millard Fillmore *who*?)

The point is, American culture (and English-speaking culture in general) has a pretty wide reach. Some of us feel a little guilty about it these days, but that doesn't change the fact that you can go pretty much anywhere in the world and find McDonald's and Coca-Cola.

But our greatest export of all is two simple letters: OK. It's the most popular word worldwide. You don't have to know English to know OK, O.K., okay, just *k*, or however else you like to say it. It's pretty much universal these days. If we ever meet some aliens, we'll probably have them saying it in a few years (unless they have something better, anyway).

But OK has a secret you may not know. It's actually just under 200 years old. As far as language goes, it's still a baby. Weirder still, though, is that it all started out as a joke.

Newspapers back in the 1830s and '40s had a fun little trend going on. They called them "comical abbreviations," and they were sort of like the LOLspeak of today. Instead of cats, though, comical abbreviations were meant to mock poor, uneducated people, because dying of malnutrition at the age of eleven in the 1800s is *totally hilarious.*

Basically, the way they worked was to take a saying, any saying, and then interpret it into, essentially, dumb hick speak. So "no go" became "know go" and "all right" became "oll wright." Then, for some reason, these words were abbreviated. For comedy, we guess? Anyway, "know go" would turn into "K.G." and "oll wright" would become "O.W."

The trend didn't last terribly long, just like we hope and pray that LOLspeak will eventually fade. One abbreviation outlasted the whole thing, however. "Oll korrect," which was shortened to "O.K." and then "OK," continued on and, in fact, was made even more popular by the campaign of President Martin Van Buren, whose nickname was "Old Kinderhook." He and his people made campaign flyers and ads reading things like "O.K. for Old Kinderhook" and "Van Buren is O.K." and solidified the word in the public consciousness. So hey, maybe the presidents got one over on Mickey Mouse. *This time.*

After a while, people sort of forgot where OK came from. Even today, we're not 100 percent certain that the origin is oll korrect (get it?), but it certainly seems to be the most likely. It's been a weird ride for OK, but at least we got over that silly abbreviation thing.

LOL, who are we kidding?

The Longest Abbreviations Ever

In theory, taking a word or phrase and condensing it into a nice, small package is supposed to make things easier. You've got acronyms, which are new words formed from abbreviations, like sonar and radar, and initialisms, which are initialized versions of much longer words or phrases, like USDA and TGIF (which actually stood for "This Gopher Is Furious" until it was hijacked by pro-weekend lobbyists back in 1952).

That doesn't really work for some abbreviations, however, such as . . .

3. ADCOMSUBORGCOMPHIBSPAC: 22 letters

It's a Naval term that stands for "Administrative Command, Amphibious Forces, Pacific Fleet Subordinate Command."

Original length: Sixty-eight letters, which means the abbreviation is one third as long.

Sanity you lose by reading it: 10 percent

2. **COMNAVSEACOMBATSYSENGSTA:** 24 letters

Another Naval term. This one means "Commander, Naval Sea Systems Combat Engineering Station."

Original length: Forty-nine letters, so the abbreviation is half as long.

Sanity you lose by reading it: 30 percent

1. **NIIOMTPLABOPARMBETZHELBETRABSBOMONIMONKONOT-DTEKHSTROMONT:** 56 letters

This is also a military term, but this time it comes from Russia. (The original Cyrillic is *Нииомтплабопармбетжелбетрабсбомонимонконот дтехстромонт*, which is actually two letters shorter. Go Russia.) Translated, it stands for "The laboratory for shuttering, reinforcement, concrete and ferroconcrete operations for composite-monolithic and monolithic constructions of the Department of the Technology of Building-assembly operations of the Scientific Research Institute of the Organization for building mechanization and technical aid of the Academy of Building and Architecture of the Union of Soviet Socialist Republics," which is funny because we've named our office bathroom the same thing.

Original length: 344 letters, making the abbreviation one sixth as long.

Sanity you lose by reading it: 100 percent

Six
Gibberish-Sounding
Sentences
That Are
Grammatically Correct

Okay, maybe the title doesn't sell this one, but we think you won't be disappointed. Since you're reading this book, we assume you have a pretty decent idea of how the English language works. You probably spent some time diagramming sentences in school. Even if you've forgotten how all of that crap works, you at least know when a sentence "looks right," correct?

Well, these linguistic brain twisters are ready to completely ruin that for you. They look nonsensical, but they actually make grammatically valid sentences, and we'll even show you how so you don't have to call up your fourth-grade English teacher while drunk and crying in the middle of the night, unable to sleep because language has just outright betrayed you.

6. "Will Will will the will to Will?"

When it's written out, this one's a little easier, but that's okay. We're just getting started. Spoken out loud, it sounds like nonsense. "Will Will will the will to Will?" Say it and see if you don't sound like you're doing some a cappella version of a techno song.

Obviously, what we're looking at here are four different versions of the word will. The first is an auxiliary verb and a form of "am." To put it differently, it'd be, "Is Will going to will the will to Will?" The second (as well as the last) is the name Will, short for William. The third is a verb form of will, meaning "to give" or "to deed." The last is the noun form of will, as in a legal document.

TRANSLATION: "Is William going to give the will to the other William?"

5. "If the police police police police, who polices the police police? Police police police police police police!"

This one isn't that complicated once you really look at it, either, but if you're not paying attention it just looks like someone started goosing the person speaking about halfway through and they started shouting for the cops. Also, it makes the word "police" stop making sense for a minute. That'll become a fixture in these, as you'll see.

In this sentence, we've got multiple parts of speech for the word police as well as a proposed organization that keeps an eye on the police from the inside, which the sentence creator, linguist Hans-Martin Gaertner, has dubbed the "police police," also known as "those rats in Internal Affairs" in every cop movie ever. Further, he surmises that there must be a group above them that also keeps an eye out, in a kind of "who watches the watchmen?" sentiment taken to a whole new level.

To make it a little easier, you can put a hyphen in when referring to the proposed organizations. Thus, it becomes "If the police-police police police, who polices the police-police? Police-police-police police police-police!" From there, it's just a matter of separating the verb form of police, "to maintain authority over," from the noun form, "the police force."

TRANSLATION: "If Internal Affairs watches the police, who watches Internal Affairs? There is a higher-tier organization in the force that observes Internal Affairs for wrongdoing!"

4. "Buffalo buffalo Buffalo buffalo buffalo buffalo Buffalo buffalo."

Chances are you're staring at that and wondering how it can even be a real sentence. It totally is, though, as we shall show you. Philosopher William J. Rapaport (which is the best philosopher name you can have) invented the sentence in 1972, presumably just to mess with people.

Your big clue here is the capitalized B on some instances of the word. Other than our latest creation, dashing super spy Buffalo Codswallop (he's a work in progress), there aren't many buffalos that require a capital B. Except, that is, for Buffalo, NY.

The other thing that can help you figure this out is a lesser-known definition of buffalo, which means "to bully." Now you might start to see how this one works.

Buffalo buffalo—that is, bisons from the city of Buffalo—are the subject of this one, and they have a tendency to bully some of the others, or, "Buffalo buffalo buffalo buffalo." But those bisons they bully also happen to be in Buffalo, and so they, too, are Buffalo buffalo.

But those Buffalo bisons being bullied also bully the other Buffalo bison in return, because they're not just going to take that crap. They're freaking gigantic. So, "Buffalo buffalo, [that] Buffalo buffalo buffalo, buffalo Buffalo buffalo [in return]." And now we have an idea that if buffalo were capable of speech, this is probably how they would sound—like giant Pokemon.

TRANSLATION: "Bisons in Buffalo, New York, like to bully other Buffalo bisons, but those same bisons bully them in return."

Lion-Eating Poet in the Stone Den

Obviously, bizarre sentences like these aren't only possible in English. All languages have their ambiguities and homonyms and fun things like that. Take, for example, a Chinese poem written by Yuen Ren Chao, titled "Lion-Eating Poet in the Stone Den," which is about a poet who likes to eat lions (because why the hell not), finds ten at the market, kills them, and brings them back to his stone den, at which point he realizes that the lions were actually decorative stone lions all along.

It's a silly poem, but what's interesting is that it's written in Classical Chinese (an old-fashioned form of written Chinese) and is perfectly legible, but when read aloud in contemporary Mandarin Chinese, all the words come out as "shi," over and over. This is due to the evolution of language from Classical Chinese (which is still widely read, but not spoken) to modern Mandarin.

So essentially, all ninety-two words of the poem sound like "shi shi shi shi shi shi shi," but can be easily read by anyone who's learned some Classical Chinese (which is basically anyone who's been through the Chinese equivalent of middle school).

It'd be like if we had a Middle English text (because Middle English is more or less readable by the average person) that read normally, but when spoken aloud was "fart" over and over, or something like that. Except our language doesn't really work the same way Chinese does, but you get what we mean.

---

3. "Can can can can can can can can can can."

This is similar to the buffalo one, but it's like someone built a keyboard that can only type the word "can" and now they're cursing you out with it. Well, screw them! We don't *need* their freaking approval. (Oh, yes we do, please like us.)

One thing you need to know about this to figure it out is that the dance called the can-can was originally just "cancan" in French, and it can actually be spelled without the hyphen at all. The second thing is another lesser known definition, like the one for buffalo, of can, which is "to throw away," like how English people say they "binned" something. You'll also need the other version, "to dismiss or fire," as in "I got canned yesterday for attempting to engage a customer in a farting contest." Last, like police-police above, this sentence proposes a place where bad can-can goes, called the "can-can can," like a garbage dump for terrible dancing.

A way you can make this easier is to reinsert the hyphen in any instances where it's referring to the dance. So, "Can can-can can can can-can can can-can." Then you swap out any instance where it's referring to dismissing something with trash. "Can can-can can trash can-can can can-can." Then you can put quotes around anything regarding the imaginary can-can dump, and replace anything regarding dismissed can-can with crap. "Crap can-can can trash 'can-can can' can-can." Who knew that French dance critics had such a hierarchy?

TRANSLATION: "Terrible can-can is still better than that which has been relegated to the can-can hall of shame."

2. "James while John had had had had had had had had had had had a better effect on the teacher."

We should have mentioned that there's not much of a difficulty curve on these. It's more like a difficulty cliff. It may help for this particular sentence to know that it actually has a little background story. James and John are two students who are asked by the teacher to describe a man who had a cold, but got over it. John said, "The man had a cold," which the teacher said was incorrect. James, on the other hand, said, "The man had had a cold." Consider it a clue. Ready to move on?

First of all, you need to realize that this sentence is screwing with you. It's missing some punctuation which, while handy, is technically optional in English since it's only intended for clarification. (Think about it this way—we don't use punctuation while speaking.) Yes, your teachers certainly taught you otherwise, and bless them for it. Just know that this is a non-standard sentence.

So what we've got is a mix of past tense and past-perfect tense, which is exactly what the teacher was trying to teach the children. "The man had a cold," while a correct sentence, does not convey that he's over it now. "The man had had a cold" tells us that the man had previously had a cold. The past-perfect, if you've forgotten, is something that happened further in the past than something that is already in the past tense, i.e., "we went to the zoo yesterday and the monkey, *who had jumped off the branch*, began flinging his poo at the glass."

Let's start breaking it down. Ignore James for now. "While John had had had" is the part we want to look at. John used "had" as his answer, so in the past-perfect tense, John had had "had."

Now back to James. "James [. . .] had had had had." James gave "had had" for his answer, so James had had "had had" in the past-perfect.

This is where it gets rough. "Had had had had a better effect on the teacher." This is actually a totally separate clause, and would normally be set apart with a semicolon. What it's saying is that James's answer, "had had," had been more impressive to the teacher (since it was right). So, in the past-perfect, "had had" had had a better effect. Okay, we're finished! Unfortunately, both James and John dropped out of school and became meth users.

TRANSLATION: "John had used 'had' in his sentence and James had used 'had had,' and James's answer impressed the teacher more because it was the correct one."

1. ▪ "That that that is that that is not is not that that is that that is is not true is not true."

Hoo boy. Yeah, we're sorry about this. This is a Lovecraftian monster in sentence form. It will drive you howling and scratching-at-the-walls mad. It's basically like someone got in a fight with alphabet soup and lost horribly. Or they had the dictionary on audiobook and it just started skipping endlessly, which is probably what hell is like for grammar Nazis.

Okay, to break this down, you need to first be aware that it's making conflicting statements. Specifically, it's using a double negative by saying that the preceding clause is untrue, then follows that up by saying that the previous claim that it's untrue is, itself, untrue. Lost? Don't worry about it. Point is, we can drop a few words here to give it a little more sense.

"That that is that that is not is not that that is that that is."

It still makes zero sense, so you have to further break it into smaller chunks. "That that is" means "something that is" or "something that exists," for example. So, "that that is that that is not" means "something that does not exist," because the "something that exists" is "that that is not," or "something that doesn't exist." Still confused? Hang on, we're bringing it around.

"That that is not is not that that is that that is."

So, we've got "something that doesn't exist is not . . . " That leaves us with "that that is that that is," which means "something that exists is something that exists," which you can reduce to "something that exists." Finally! "A thing that does not exist is not a thing that does exist." Cool. That kind of makes sense. Except we've got that double negative we left off from earlier to add back in.

The first "is not true" means that the statement we just wrenched out of that mess is incorrect. So, according to this sentence, a thing that exists is the same as something that doesn't exist. That's obviously not true, as confirmed when we add the second "not true" back in, because something that's real and something that isn't aren't the same thing at all. Duh. Er, we think. So, yeah, even though the sentence now makes a kind of sense, you still have to get philosophical and think about it, which is just kind of cruel. Sorry!

TRANSLATION: "It's incorrect to say that a thing which is real (an ape) is the same as a thing which is fake (the sasquatch), because that is an untrue statement: things that do and do not exist are totally different."

The -Gry Puzzle

Speaking of word puzzles, that reminds us of a little riddle. There are three words in the English language that end with the suffix *-gry*. We'll give you two: Hungry and angry. What's the third?

Give up? Well, you should, because there isn't an answer. Those are the only two. In fact, -gry is one of those rare English suffixes that is, well, rare. (Another is the *-mt* ending, found in dreamt, which gets used nowhere else.)

We didn't come up with the puzzle and we're not just trying to screw with you. It's a real "riddle" that gets passed around all the time, especially on the Internet.

Basically, it's an urban legend that there's a third word that ends with -gry, because if there were there'd be a game with it plus an animal in the title to stick with Hungry Hungry Hippos and Angry Birds. Some people have come up with clever non-answers, but it's basically just a way to keep someone busy while you steal their wallet or whatever.

Ten
Everyday Words
That Have No Rhyme

It's a popular and commonly repeated factoid that there are only four words in the English language that don't have words that rhyme with them. We're here today to tell you that fact is crap. There are, in fact, thousands of words without rhymes. When's the last time you heard a rhyme for "conversational?"

Of course, in the modern age, there are only three reasons to even worry about rhymes. You're probably not a starving poet or a cheesy songwriter, so we're going to assume you're trying to brush up on your rap flow so you can show off while freestyling. As such, we've included a handy mini-thesaurus of much easier rhyme words so you can adjust your lyrics accordingly.

Now, to be clear, we're looking at perfect rhymes—that is, words that are exact rhymes, like fall and ball. Slant rhymes, like argue and corkscrew, don't count. And please keep in mind that in certain accents and dialects, it's very possible that these words rhyme with something. Hell, you can put a ton of marbles in your mouth and then *everything rhymes*. We found that out the hard way.

10. Bulb

If you're an electrician working on a rhyming couplet about changing out lights, we've got bad news for you. It turns out that there are no rhymes for bulb, which means that you'll be left wanting when you need to follow up your line about the heart-wrenching sorrow of a blown-out light.

WORDS THAT MIGHT WORK BETTER: Ball (rhymes with fall, tall, squall . . .), globe (rhymes with lobe, probe, robe . . .), and nub (rhymes with stub, grub, pub . . .)

9. Wolf

There's a reason that we had Auggie Doggie and Doggie Daddy instead of Simon Wolf and his dad, Ted Wolf or whatever. It seems there are no clever matchings for wolf, except for more wolves, and that's just asking to get mauled (or turned into an ironic T-shirt that bored people write reviews for on Amazon.com).

> **WORDS THAT MIGHT WORK BETTER:** Dog (rhymes with log, smog, cog . . .), mutt (rhymes with great words like smut, butt, nut . . .), and pooch (rhymes with hooch, and you really don't need any other rhymes than that).

8. Iron

We are so sorry for this, Mr. Stark, but if you ever try to write a catchy Iron Man theme song (instead of just borrowing Black Sabbath's song, which doesn't even try to rhyme iron), you're going to have a really tough time. But hey, you're rich. You can buy your way into the dictionary. Coming soon: Hiron -n. The act of foolishly doubting Tony Stark's fortune.

> **WORDS THAT MIGHT WORK BETTER:** Steel (rhymes with feel, real, zeal . . .), hard (rhymes with guard, bard, lard . . .), and ferrous (rhymes with heiress, Paris, and embarrass, all things that Tony Stark is more than capable of doing in a single night).

7. Pint

It's kind of incredible, considering the insane number of old-fashioned drinking songs and dirty limericks and what-have-you out there, that we've never noticed that nothing rhymes with pint. In fact, it almost seems downright impossible. We're sort of surprised the alcoholics of the world didn't just resort to making up words so that they could get back to drinking.

WORDS THAT MIGHT WORK BETTER: Mug (rhymes with pug, lug, bug. . .), glass (rhymes with ass, and we might as well stop there, because that's as good as it gets), and stein (rhymes with fine, line, and brine, as in pickled, as in your liver).

6. Gulf

All of the amateur poetry in the world came to a screeching halt after the Deepwater Horizon disaster when they simultaneously realized that nothing rhymes with gulf. Suddenly, none of the hackneyed Facebook status poets could come up with a thing. Unfortunately, the fact made them so upset that they wrote a crappy screed about that instead, and the world kept on turning.

WHAT MIGHT WORK BETTER: Bay (rhymes with play, stay, tray . . .), cove (rhymes with dove, stove, wove . . .), and harbor (rhymes with barber, so you'd better find a way to work one in there).

5. Elbow

It is often said that you cannot lick your own elbow, which is usually followed up with, "hah hah, you just tried to do it." (We've heard it a million times and we just tried it yet again, even though we're the ones who typed it, so don't feel too bad if you did.) Unfortunately, you can't rhyme elbow, either, which makes us say screw elbows, who needs 'em. We'll just start doing everything with arms completely outstretched.

WHAT MIGHT WORK BETTER: Bend (rhymes with lend, send, append . . .), joint (rhymes with point and a lot of other compound words that include point and joint), crook (rhymes with look, book, and unhook, as in bras, and now we remember what we need elbows for).

4. Empty

Writing a future hit country song about riding across the desert in your big, dusty old pickup truck? Well, when you pass the last exit for 200 miles, make sure to fill up your tank, because there's no way to rhyme empty. The good news is, that will still leave you plenty of room for further lyrics about your terrible ex.

WHAT MIGHT WORK BETTER: Bare (rhymes with hare, scare, pair . . .), dry (rhymes with lie, fly, and cry, all of which fit well with the desert theme, imaginary country musician), and depleted (rhymes with seated, heated, cheated, and now we're practically writing the song for you).

3. Liquid

Well, this one just screws everyone. No rhymes for liquid means no couplets about sports drinks, no limericks about the states of matter, and no old-fashioned dirges about peeing. You can get close with "squid," and they live in liquid, which is highly convenient. Unfortunately, unless you're writing a rollicking sea shanty, there's not much room for squid in most cases.

WHAT MIGHT WORK BETTER: Water (rhymes with blotter, daughter, otter . . .), juice (rhymes with noose, spruce, sluice . . .), and fluid (rhymes with druid, and that already sounds like an amazing masterpiece).

2. Angel

Holy crap, you mean to tell us that after thousands of years of religion and hymns and songs and poems, there are *no rhymes for angel*? It almost seems like a cruel joke. What's your game, God? Are you playing us for some sort of chumps?

WHAT MIGHT WORK BETTER: Seraph (rhymes with sheriff, tariff, serif . . .), divinity (rhymes with trinity, affinity, infinity . . .), and cherub (rhymes with Arab, scarab, and carob, which is like chocolate, so it's sort of heavenly, except it tastes like burnt poop, so, you know, maybe not).

1. Month

We have twelve of them in a year, and yet nothing rhymes with them. Worse, several of the actual month names are pretty difficult to rhyme, even if you fudge them. We seem to recall a song in grade school with the months of the year, but even then, they didn't really rhyme, except a few did with each other. Why do you mock us, calendar?

WHAT MIGHT WORK BETTER: We don't even have a freaking synonym for month. It's just month. What can you say instead? "Set, named thirty-day period of time"? Then you sound like an asshole *and* you're not going to fit that into anything, ever. Congratulations.

Three Words That *Actually* Rhyme with Orange

It's commonly believed that there are no words that rhyme with orange. Meanwhile, plenty of pseudo-rhymes have been suggested, like "door hinge" and "four-inch," but those aren't exact rhymes.

But, for the record, there are three words that really *do* rhyme with orange. The first is the name of a hill in—where else—Wales. The Blorenge is a large hill in southeastern Wales that is pronounced exactly like orange with a *bl-* in front of it. So if you brought an orange to The Blorenge, you'd automatically become a poet (and totally know it).

The second word that rhymes with orange is Gorringe, an uncommon surname found in the Sussex area of England. There's even a ridge off the coast of Portugal called Gorringe Ridge, named after the man who discovered it, Captain Henry Gorringe.

The third is sporange, an archaic alternative for sporangium, which is the little container that spores come in.

So if you really want to throw down with some fools at your next rap battle, you could toss out something like, "Going to The Blorenge with my sporange to fix a door hinge and share a four-inch orange with Lauren Gorringe." Make sure to drop the mic after that. We hear that's cool.

The
Most Common
Words in the
English Language

If asked to pick the most used word in your vocabulary (assuming that the person asking wouldn't actually bother to check), what answer would you give? For us, it'd be something like "spackle," probably. We talk about spackling a lot. It just comes up naturally in conversation (by which we mean we constantly yell out "spackle" while talking to other people in hopes that it will become a saying).

But what if you could ask the English language itself, assuming the English language were personified (in our minds as a guy named Steve who really enjoys cold winter nights curled up on the couch) and could respond to you? Well, good news for you (bad news for Steve), you don't have to.

Oxford Dictionaries, the superheroes who compile the *Oxford English Dictionary*, have created a giant collection of written English that they call the Oxford English Corpus, which kind of makes it sound like a very posh zombie. It's made up of over 2 billion words and comes from sources as diverse as literature to chat rooms.

Using the magic of technology, Oxford has combed through this database of language and come up with the most common words in English. Unfortunately for all of you (meaning us) holding out hope that the most popular word was some underdog like "Octopussy," we've got bad news.

The most regularly used words in English are actually kind of boring. "The," "be," "to," "of," "and," "a," "in," "that," "have," and "I" make up the top ten. Man, we are freaking dull. German and French probably have all kinds of cool words at the top. Oxford Dictionaries even points out that if you know a mere 7,000 words and their standard variations (for tenses and the like) you've *already covered 90 percent of everyday English.* Keep in mind that the average adult has a vocabulary of about 15,000 words, which means we only use less than half of that the vast majority of the time.

But wait! Oxford Dictionaries also compiled what they call the top "content words," i.e., the good stuff, conveniently split into nouns, verbs, adjectives, and more (but they're not very interesting, so we're skipping those). All right, let's see how spackle has done in our three categories!

The Ten Most Common Nouns in the English Language

We begin with nouns, those things that are things.

10. Hand

Of all the body's parts, the ones we use to directly manipulate our environment are apparently the ones we talk about the most. Go figure. (Hopefully you don't use those parts *down there* to manipulate your environment, otherwise you're probably reading this from jail.)

9. Life

Life: it's what we're all doing here, trapped in this world of crazy sons of bitches and occasional relief in the form of attractive people and cute babies and kittens/puppies and stuff. Considering that almost 100 percent of literature is about people's lives, whether fiction or fact, this makes total sense.

8. World

And hey, that dovetails nicely with this one. Everyone you know is on the same world as you. Crazy, huh? Except for those people who slip into the

Other Worlds, anyway. Back here, we think they disappeared, but no. They can just never come home again, because they're in a dimension where the CSA won the Civil War or something. What were we talking about?

7. Man

Will you look at that? Man comes in at number seven while "woman" doesn't show up until number fourteen, and we had to cut this off at ten because we have a word count, buster. Talk about subtle sexism. It actually does make an interesting statement about our patriarchal society throughout thousands of years of language. It's okay, ladies. We're working on doing better.

6. Thing

What do you call a thing when you don't know what the thing that thing is? Forget about the *f*-word, thing is easily more versatile. Although, substituting it back into the first sentence there, maybe we're wrong. Anyway, a thing can be a mysterious figure or even just a nameless concept (or, yes, *those things*, jail readers), so yeah, it is a thing (see?) that pops up a lot (shut up, jail readers).

5. Day

Being as we're not a nocturnal species and everything, it does follow that we'd spend a lot of time talking about, y'know, the daytime, which in this age means either going to work, staying home and watching talk shows, or whatever else instead of hunting and gathering, but it's still when we get the most stuff done. (More specifically, we get the most done in the first half-hour of waking up and just coast from there.)

4. Way

We'd like to think this popped up because of people talking about the Fastball song "The Way" (even before it was actually released, to boot), but it's probably because of all the writing we've done about how to get places and stuff like that. Or maybe it's just a whole bunch of people using it in that annoying '80s/early '90s "no way" "yes way" fashion.

3. Year

Years are pretty much the only meaningful time measurement we have as humans. Decades are so long we don't really mark their passage (except for nostalgia purposes, which is a relatively new phenomenon) and we rarely live a whole century. Years, though, we can dig that. Most importantly, we measure our age in years, usually while openly weeping and recounting our glory days.

2. Person

Well, hey, if we didn't write about other people, stuff would be pretty boring. We're not all René Descartes up in here, right? Right. (For anyone who doesn't know what that means, it's just a reference that people who desperately want to seem smart throw out sometimes.) *The Lord of the Rings* without other people would just be some dopey hobbit taking a really long walk. The Bible without other people would just be God hanging around for a few thousand years.

1. Time

Isn't it kind of beautiful, in a poetic way, that the most commonly written about subject is time? No one can escape it, and yet we still struggle against it, like it's the villain in the superhero story that is mankind. It's like . . . wait a second. Time, person, year . . . were we just on the receiving end of some viral marketing from *Time* magazine, or are they that in touch with the collective unconscious?

The Ten Most Common Adjectives in the English Language

And now for adjectives, the things that describe the things.

10. Old

Age is one of the easiest descriptors we've got. That old man. His old, busted pickup. Even things that are relatively new can be old, like if your town has two animal jock strap stores, the first one will always be "the *old* animal jock strap store," even if they opened within months of each other.

9. Other

Unfortunately, this is probably not referring to The Others on *Lost*. Or maybe it is, hell. Everyone and their grandma had a theory about that show, after all. Anyway, other is a nice, broad term for "not this one." You wanna have some real fun? Get into a debate with a philosopher on the nature of "the other." Bring a pillow.

8. Own

Ownership is nine-tenths of the law, but it only gets you to the eighth spot on this list. Possession, of course, is one of the first things we learn as children (usually by way of squawking *"That's mine!"*) and is a very important concept in our capitalist society, fellow Western pig. (It's also a very important subject to young girls in '70s-era horror movies, but that's another story.)

7. Little

Size is another great, clear descriptive term. When something is little, it's undersized or trivial (stop giggling, please). It can also be diminutive or cute (okay, seriously, we can hear you smirking). Obviously, little things will come up frequently in any sort of writing . . . but mostly in amateur porn writing! Boom! We were the ones giggling all along! That's called a plot twist.

6. Great

Some are born great, some achieve greatness, and some are, like, "What's so great about being great anyway? Screw that, I have Netflix to catch up on." It makes sense that you'd see this one a lot, from Alexander the Great to that really great Reuben you had last week. We like to talk about the good things we come across, at least until we get old and cranky.

5. Long

Now here's a word that describes us, if you know what we mean. Super long. Long-winded, that is! (But seriously, our self-esteem hinges on you believing the implied meaning there, too, so be a sport, all right? Thanks.) Anyway, long car trips, long days, and live long and prosper. Length is, y'know, good for measuring and stuff. Of course it's common.

4. Last

The last of anything has a bitter kind of sadness (unless it's the last of a string of kicks to the groin, that is), so it becomes a powerful concept to human-kind, especially with that whole mortality thing we struggle with. (Well, you may struggle with it. We've firmly come to grips with the fact that we're going to die in a burning gas station restroom in six years.)

3. First

Of course, the only thing more interesting than the last of something is the first. A baby's first steps, first words, and first tooth are something worth writing about, compared to the last of those things. (We can't all have exciting final days.) Would you rather be first in line for something, or last in line? (Assuming the something isn't something like a dunking booth filled with eels.)

2. New

And following that up nicely is new. New things are fun and shiny. New loves, new socks, a new roll of toilet paper—all of these things make us happy. When someone asks how your day is going, they want to hear about what's new and exciting. Even if you're having a crappy, terrible day, at least it's something different from yesterday, right?

1. Good

Well, hey. Maybe human existence isn't all bad, because apparently we really love talking about good things. Or maybe we just keep the bad things all bottled up inside until we spontaneously combust, anyway, but that seems unlikely considering the lack of spontaneous combustion cases following the dawn of reality television. We'll hold out hope that things are generally good.

The Ten Most Common Verbs in the English Language

Finally, verbs, the things that thing the things.

10. See

Sight is our primary sense as human beings (good luck finding your way to the bathroom in the dark by smell—wait, please don't make your bathroom findable by smell at all, actually), so we obviously use a lot of words associated with it. For example, we once saw Meryl Streep eating a piece of pizza she found in the garbage. Actually, that probably wasn't *really* her, but who can say for sure?

9. Take

To acquire, usually by force. Human domination asserts itself outright. If you want something, take it. If someone stops you, club them with that aurochs bone you found last full moon. Okay, sometimes you don't forcibly take things, like medicine or, our personal favorite, a nap (also *probably* a poop, we hope), but you get our point.

8. Know

Knowledge is power, and if you bought this book with that in mind, we apologize in advance for not giving you super strength. We tried, but there's only so much that The Man will let us get away with. Still, as we mentioned in the Introduction, human knowledge and its conveyance is one of the most important skills we've developed, and so it naturally makes up a large bulk of our writing.

7. Go

Being on the move, considered a negative trait in the modern era, has its roots way, way back in human history (when we were nomads, everywhere was Grand Central Station, and the bathroom, too), and now, after millennia of telling people, *"Go! Run! Save yourself!"* we've proven our dedication to telling people what to do, just like our mothers.

6. Make

Since we have very versatile organs for manipulating things (oh, for the last time, we mean *hands*) and advanced brains that allow us to conceive of new and interesting ways to do stuff, we've gotten pretty good at making various things. Food, computers, unicycles (come on, *that* is inspired design) . . . truly, we are a species of creators. Mostly of porn, but we do what we can.

5. Get

To acquire, but not necessarily by force. A great poet once said, "[F-word] [derogatory term for women], get money." (Sorry, we have editorial standards to uphold.) While the presentation may be off-color, the message itself is not. We are here to procreate and gather resources, after all, making it the perfect summation of human existence. Q.E.D. (We've always wanted to say that.)

4. Say

This one shouldn't be too surprising when you consider that about 90 percent of all dialogue in a novel is followed by "so-and-so said." Humans, by their very nature, have a lot to say (some more than others, noisy office-mates), which is handy because we'd be sitting around quietly twiddling our thumbs our whole lives otherwise.

3. Do

Now we've reached the quintessential verbs. We basically don't have a choice in these, since we kind of meet the requirements by existing at all. Like do: every thing you've ever done (see, there it is) is just you *doing* something. Even sitting still, breathing heavily, and thinking of Elvis is an action that you're committed to doing. You cannot escape do. Accept your fate.

2. Have

Likewise, have is unavoidable. You always possess something, whether you're Donald Trump (in which case you possess a stupid face and an annoying demeanor) or totally bankrupt (in which case you possess either a heart of gold or a crippling drug addiction, whichever). Whether it's your health, your dashing good looks, or your overwhelming sense of gas-related anxiety, you always own something.

1. Be

Now we're getting downright philosophical. Is, are, was, were, and all those various forms of be included, we've basically got the lynchpin of the English language right here. Everything *is* (and no, we will not help you redefine it, former President Clinton), in some form or another. So yeah, we can kind of see why this would be the most common verb we've got.

The Most Common Words in the United States Constitution

It's fine and dandy to note the most common words in a general selection of texts, but what about more specialized documents? You can learn a lot about a manuscript by examining the words that are in it. For example, the most common words in this book are all references to bodily functions/parts and, strangely, George Clinton and the Parliament Funkadelic.

Since it's in style to argue about what the Founding Fathers had in mind for the United States these days, why don't we find out exactly what they intended and break down the most common words in the original Constitution?

Leaving out boring linking words, the word Constitution itself, and other cruft, the most recurring words, in order, are State (131 times), United (54 times), President (34 times), Law (also 34 times), Office (yet again, 34 times), Congress (29 times), and Person (22 times). So they meant for us to have separate (but united) states, a congress, offices that would have purview over certain aspects of the government, laws, a president, and, of course, a whole mess of people. Mystery solved!

Wait, there's nothing about religion or guns or fat people? Looks like we have to settle all that crap with cage matches. Sorry, everyone.

Three
of the
Largest Publications
Ever Created

Obviously, we're not talking about the longest words here. We already did that one. If you didn't know that because you're skipping around, shame on you. You're just trying to get to the twist at the end of the book. To throw you off the scent, however, we're including it right here instead: You did it. You killed all those people and then gave yourself amnesia to forget. You've been living a lie, and now the revelation comes in a totally unassuming humorous reference book. Or does it? Maybe you're just insane and these words aren't really here. Let's be honest, you've been losing your grip these last few months. Maybe you *should* go away for a while. It might be better. For everyone. Only for a few weeks, and then you'll feel loads better. Just think about it, okay?

Ahem, now that that's covered, what were we talking about? Oh, right, large words. We're looking at the biggest, grandest words . . . like, size-wise. As in words that take up the greatest amount of space.

3. ▪ Massive Books

For nearly 350 years, *The Klencke Atlas* was the largest book in the world. Created by Dutch cartographers as a gift to King Charles II of England, the atlas is about 5 feet and 9 inches tall, 3½ feet wide, and over 6 feet wide when fully opened. Each page is a massive, hand-drawn map—quite a feat for the 1660s. We're lucky to properly doodle directions to the nearest McDonald's without throwing in a turn that doesn't exist, and we have access to Google Maps. Now, to be fair, an atlas doesn't have a whole lot of printed words, but it does have some, for labels and the like, so we'll count it.

"But hang on—it *was* the largest book?" you might be saying. Yep, was, because in 2012, Millennium House of Australia one-upped it with their own giant atlas titled *Earth Platinum,* which measures 6 feet tall and 4½ feet wide. Instead of just hand-drawn maps, however, *Earth Platinum* includes enormous satellite pictures of the Earth and extremely high-resolution professional digital photography of various regions and landscapes.

But if we're going to talk about huge books, we'd be remiss if we didn't mention *Bhutan: A Visual Odyssey Across the Last Himalayan Kingdom.* It doesn't have any words, as it's a visual exhibit book meant to showcase very high-end digital photography taken in Bhutan (obviously). However, it is still the largest book in the world at 7 by 5 feet, making it almost the size of a regulation ping-pong table. Oh, and it costs $10,000, so you might as well use it as a diving board, too, while you're at it.

2. Enormous Signs

Nobody likes ads, but at least billboards give you something to look at in traffic (besides the attractive person in the next car over, who is likely to shoot you the bird—or just shoot you—when they catch you looking, if your luck is anything like ours). And while the words on billboards have gotten larger to accommodate speedier traffic, the billboards themselves are more or less the same size. Unless you count the enormous ones that people have made for the sake of having "the biggest," that is.

You may be unaware that the Hollywood sign in L.A. originally read "Hollywoodland," and you may be further unaware that it also lit up and flashed, because it was actually a 400-foot-long, 50-foot-high giant advertisement for a housing community of the same name. The Hollywood sign was originally only intended to last about eighteen months, but people liked it so much that they kept it around and, eventually, dropped the flashing lights and the "land" part, reducing the length down to 350 feet. (Also worth noting is that, far from its current state, the Hollywood sign was practically trashed by the '70s, with missing and broken letters, and had to be completely rebuilt, which had the added consequence of lowering the height to its current 45 feet.)

But it's technically beat out by the Paddy Power sign featured on Cleeve Hill in Cheltenham, England, for a week during the 2010 Gold Cup race (American readers: It's horses, not cars). Paddy Power, if you're not familiar, is a massive Irish betting company (which is legal over there) with a name that might be slightly offensive to those with Irish ancestors, but not at all to actual Irish people, who apparently don't really give a damn. As a method of advertising its services during the race, the company temporarily (though they had intended for it to be permanent, they were required to remove it after the race) erected the sign, a parody of the Hollywood sign, on Cleeve Hill, overlooking the Cheltenham Racecourse. At 50 feet high, it was just slightly taller than the modern Hollywood sign (it was the same height as the original, though). It was, however, quite a bit shorter lengthwise, at only 270 feet long.

1. ▪ Holy Effin' Huge Geoglyphs

We'll go ahead and get this out of the way: Geoglyphs are designs carved or otherwise built into the ground and intended to be viewable from the air, such as the massive Nazca Lines of Peru or the thousands of crop circles made around the world each year. (By people, we mean, not aliens. The aliens only make the really silly ones.)

Nowadays, we've run out of fun ways to create images of giant people or genitals on the ground and have resorted to more interesting ways of communicating with clouds. (Why don't they ever reply to us? They could spell out, like, "Hey, thanks!" or something at least. The freakin' jerks.) You know, things like tremendous words that birds and dragons and whatever else lives in the sky can look at and say, "You know what? Those humans are all right."

We'll start with the oldest. Built in 1965 by Allan Hoare with a commercial road grader, the Nullarbor Plain Readymix logo is exactly what it sounds like: A giant Readymix (a brand of concrete) logo carved into the middle of the desert. Although very faint today, the symbol could, at one point, reportedly be seen from space. It's about 2 miles wide and and 1 mile tall (though the letters themselves are only about a mile wide and 800 feet tall). Hold on, though, because we're just getting started.

In the Atacama Desert in Chile, poet Raul Zurita created the world's largest poem back in 1993. It's only four words, "ni pena ni miedo" (meaning "neither shame nor fear"), but it, too, is approximately 2 miles wide (which is apparently the secret sauce for geoglyphs) and 1,500 feet at the tallest point, or about twice as big as the Readymix letters.

Then, there's Futaisi Island, just off the coast of the United Arab Emirates. In 2011, Sheikh Hamad Bin Hamdan Al Nahyan, a former ruler of Adu Dhabi and full-time massively, insanely rich guy, had his own name, HAMAD, carved into the island's surface, basically for hell of it. The letters are a bit less than two miles wide and a bit more than half a mile tall. Craziest of all, the letters are also giant irrigation ditches and fill up with ocean water that spills into them.

Finally, near Austin, Texas, a homeowner named Luecke has deforested part of his land to spell out his own name. The letters are about 2½ miles wide and about ½ a mile tall, making them the largest letters on earth. Reportedly, the letters were created for two reasons: The hell of it, and to mess with aircraft flying overhead. Sure, it may seem like it's a pretty normal sign of mental instability for the area (you ever been to Austin?), but the kicker is that NASA is actually now using the letters to calibrate space-based photography equipment due to their size and visibility. So, you know, keep that in mind next time you make something ridiculous in your yard. NASA might need it for something.

Three
of the
Smallest Publications
Ever Created

Now let's flip the script and get tiny. Making huge sets of letters is one thing. Making them so tiny that they're practically invisible? That's just insanity, and we know insanity. And little things, too, sadly. Let's not talk about that, and just get started.

3. ▪ Adorably Tiny Handwritten Books

Little versions of big things are great. Tell us you wouldn't keep a miniature giraffe or elephant as a pet if you could. There's nothing about that that wouldn't be amazing, except for the mini heaps of wild animal dung dotting your carpet. We love kittens and puppies and, yes, baby sloths, too, for the same reason. It's something we already like, but tiny and cute. Turns out, that totally follows through for adorable, little books, too. Aww!

Miniature books are actually kind of a thing. They were particularly popular in the nineteenth century because they're easy to carry and difficult to confiscate. Need a spy manual so you don't forget which button on your pen records audio, and which causes it to explode? Get a miniature book, and also, you might consider a different career if this is a frequent issue.

There's even a Miniature Book Society that is full of nothing but people who collect books that are 3 inches or less in length, width, or thickness. If you shop around online, you can find hundreds of books, some rare collectibles, in itty-bitty format. Now that we have eBooks and stuff, the size concerns aren't so much a thing, but dang, they are amazing little art pieces all the same.

Then, there's the actual smallest paper book. At less than 1 millimeter square, it's about the size of Abe Lincoln's schnoz on a penny. The book is a reproduction of Anton Chekhov's short story "A Chameleon," and covers 30 tiny pages along with 3 wee baby illustrations. You just wanna pinch its little bindings. The book was created completely by hand by Russian micro-miniature artist Anatoly Konenko, because he just likes making very small books (as well as other nigh-microscopic pieces of art).

2. Super-Cute Nano Printed Books

These are the littlest things that we might reasonably consider a "book," per se. They don't have pages, but are instead inscribed on tiny silicon wafers, so you can argue whether or not they're books the same way that people argue whether eBooks are "real books" or not. (Hi, eBook people! We love you.)

Still, the exceptionally miniscule Technion Nano Bible is the world's smallest reproduction of this book about a dude who created the world. (It's pretty intense, we hear.) Featuring the entirety of the Old Testament, it's about the size of a pinhead (or half a grain of sugar) at 0.5 millimeters square, and was created by scientists at the Israeli Institute of Technology in 2007 using an ion beam. Amazingly, it only took an hour and a half for the actual printing. If you want one, too bad. The former Pope Benedict XVI owns the only copy.

Finally, we have the tiniest of the tiny. The official smallest book in the world is *Teeny Ted from Turnip Town*, an original work written by Malcolm Douglas Chaplin and created by his brother, Robert Chaplin. Much like the Technion Bible, Teeny Ted was printed onto a silicon wafer, but a much, much smaller one (you need a scanning electron microscope to even see the book, much less read it). It's 70 microns by 100 microns, or 0.07 mm by 0.1 mm, or really, really stupidly small. Manufactured at the Nano Imaging Facility at Simon Fraser University, it has been certified by Guinness World Records as the smallest book ever. It even has its own little ISBN. As of October 2012, the Chaplin Brothers are working on producing a "large print" (i.e., human-sized) edition for everyone without Superman vision.

1. ▪ Eensy Little Words

You want to go even smaller because your sense of dignity is still coming up short, you say? Yeah, we can go smaller, and not for any reason that has to do with personal pride or a deep sense of bodily shame. Our first stop takes us back to the storied year of 1989, when everything was finally getting out of the bananas-town era that was the '80s and ushering us into the slightly less insane '90s. (And we do mean *slightly*.) Back then, one of the big names in science and technology was a little company that's all but disappeared today—IBM.

In September of 1989, IBM researcher Don Eigler became the first human to ever directly manipulate an atom. Two months later, he decided to really flex his new godlike powers (okay, not really) to manipulate thirty-five xenon atoms into spelling out I-B-M. Hey, it's not much creativity-wise, but as far as quantum science goes, it was a huge deal. And, with each letter clocking in at a mere five nanometers, or 0.000005 millimeters (a.k.a. so small it doesn't even mean anything to us anymore, so let's just nod our heads and move on), it was the tiniest writing in the history of mankind.

That is until 2009, when researchers at Stanford University got even crazier and created the world's first *subatomic* writing (meaning smaller than atoms, meaning what are we even talking about anymore because holy crap that's mind-blowingly small). To achieve this insane, outrageous feat, the scientists actually had to manipulate an atom's quantum wave to holographically show the letters *S* and *U* (for Stanford University, or possibly "Suck it, U guys"). If you don't understand what that means, that's okay. Just know that it's extremely cool and *probably* won't destroy the universe and everything will be fine. The letters were 0.3 nanometers tall, or about four times smaller than the IBM letters. It's small. That's what we're saying. It's super, incredibly small, and it'll warp your brain if you try to think about it too much, so just turn the TV back on for a while, and if you see any science books coming, run in the other direction.

The **Seven**
Longest Speeches
Ever Given

No speech is longer than the one you have to sit through when you graduate, except for maybe the one that interrupts your favorite TV show. (Pre-empt the next show, for crap's sake. No one watches it anyway.) Or that's how it seems. Turns out there are lots of speeches that have gone on *way* longer. Apparently there are some superhuman people out there who not only can talk for hours at a time, but can even do it without having to pee, eat, or sleep. Either that or they let loose behind their desk/podium in a secret jar or something.

7. ■ Hugo Chavez

Former Venezuelan President Hugo Chavez, otherwise known as "that guy who really didn't like the United States," served as leader in his country for over a decade, and in that time he gave *a lot* of speeches. He was a man who wasn't shy about talking, so much so that he had his own show on Venezuelan TV called *Aló Presidente*. It was basically a talk show starring, you know, a head of state of a major country instead of a wacky comedian or older actress.

The thing about *Aló Presidente* is that, while it had a set start time (11:00 A.M.), it didn't have a set end, and since Chavez had control of, well, basically everything in Venezuela, he could go on for as long as he liked. And he did. Frequently. In 2007, President Chavez gave an eight-hour speech on *Aló Presidente* on pretty much everything he could think of, mostly focusing on policy and affairs, but occasionally breaking into song or telling jokes. Woof.

In 2011, however, *Aló Presidente* was put on hold while Chavez recovered from surgery. In January 2012, he came back with a bang, giving a nearly ten-hour-long televised speech in front of the Venezuelan National Assembly, after having cancer surgery just a few months prior. He may have been kind of a jerk, but he had some endurance.

6. William Proxmire

A U.S. Senator from Wisconsin, William Proxmire would have made today's fiscal conservatives proud. In a September 1981 session of the Senate, Proxmire opted to filibuster a bill to raise the public debt ceiling. That's the exact same thing that the U.S. Congress has been fighting about, over and over, for the last few years. (Remember? They bitched at each other so long that America's credit rating went from AAA to AA+ because the worldwide financial community was concerned that we were too dumb to figure out how to run our own country anymore.)

That debt ceiling increase, which would have raised the maximum to $1 trillion (for comparison, it's at $16.394 trillion as of 2013), made Proxmire and his fellow debt-hating politicians decide to try to put a stop to the bill. Senator Proxmire filibustered (meaning he gave a speech to hold off voting on the bill) for an amazing sixteen hours and twelve minutes. It passed anyway, but Proxmire apparently just wanted to tell everyone how mad he was. For sixteen hours.

It ended up biting him in the ass, too, because his critics were quick to point out that he cost the taxpayers a boatload of cash by keeping the Senate open all night. (Turns out those lights and security guards cost money.) But before you start grumbling about those evil Republicans and their kvetching about the national debt—Proxmire was a Democrat.

5. Robert La Follette Sr.

Let's get old school. Way back in May 1908, another U.S. Senator from Wisconsin, Robert La Follette Sr., filibustered a bill that would allow the Federal Reserve to loan out money to troubled banks. You might recognize that ability of the Federal Reserve from recent history, because it's exactly what happened with the 2008 TARP bank bailouts. So, y'know, spoiler alert: La Follette's filibuster didn't work.

Regardless, he didn't like the idea of banks being able to be kept alive on the taxpayer's dime (this sounding familiar?) and so he stood in front of the Senate and filibustered for eighteen hours and twenty-three minutes. He might have gone on even longer, too, but he got thirsty.

You see, Senator La Follette asked his fellows on the Senate floor if one of them would bring him some milk mixed with raw eggs (people in the early 1900s ate like Rocky Balboa, apparently). They did, and he was able to continue speaking. He continued requesting the drink throughout the evening, but upon drinking one of the glasses, La Follette grimaced and ran off to vomit. Turns out whoever brought him the egg-milk had actually mixed ptomaine (basically, gunk from a decayed animal corpse) into the concoction, which made La Follette so ill he couldn't continue his filibuster. And you thought politicians were assholes *today*.

4. Wayne Morse

Well hey, it's another U.S. Senator, this time from Oregon. But he was born in Wisconsin, so apparently Wisconsinites love to talk. Senator Wayne Morse was a bit of an outsider, highly outspoken, and kind of crazy. After leaving the Republican Party in 1953, Morse switched over to Independent status and basically decided he didn't have to take anyone's crap anymore.

In an April 1953 session, Wayne Morse filibustered the Submerged Lands Act of 1953 for an incredible twenty-two hours and twenty-six minutes. Morse wasn't a fan of the bill, which gave all the coastal tidelands (that is, the area between high and low tides) within three miles of a state's shores to those corresponding states. He felt that the land belonged to the public, and not just the states that happened to be sitting on them (and the large oil companies who had heavily invested in the various states' governments).

Why would anyone give a crap about tidelands, you ask? Well, this is another piece of legislation that's become super-important today. Offshore lands tend to be lousy with oil, just ripe for the taking. You know, "drill, baby, drill," the Deepwater Horizon oil spill, all that fun stuff.

But the trick with the Submerged Lands Act came a few months later, when Congress came back and passed the Outer Continental Shelf Lands Act, which gave them ownership of everything *beyond* those tidelands. Therefore, the states got some land they could use for offshore drilling, but the feds got a whole lot more. So in a roundabout sort of way, Senator Morse kind of got what he was asking for. Too bad he couldn't take back the almost entire day he spend talking about it.

3. ■ Alfonse D'Amato

Maybe it's not the Wisconsin thing that we should be looking at. Maybe it's just being a U.S. Senator that causes people to talk for extraordinary lengths of time. Now, to be fair, filibustering in the House of Representatives hasn't been allowed since 1842, otherwise they would be in this list as well. We propose the possibility that super-talkative people just avoid running for the House for that very reason, though.

In 1986, one of the last cases where the threat of a filibuster turned into an actual filibuster, Senator Alfonse D'Amato of New York protested a routine budget bill. His beef with it? It cut out military funding for a training jet produced by a manufacturer located in his state. Talk about sour grapes. D'Amato's filibuster lasted twenty-three hours and thirty minutes, nearly a whole damned day. In the end, D'Amato's filibuster only led to a stay of execution. Not long after, the program was canceled for good and the factory closed down. (In the government's defense, the jet—the Fairchild T-46A—had a host of issues, which is why they wanted to kill it in the first place.)

D'Amato is also famous for another filibuster he held in 1992. It was long, at fifteen hours and fourteen minutes, but obviously D'Amato had already outdone himself there. It was famous because it has been, to date, the last solo filibuster performed in the U.S. Senate. There have been others since, of course, but performed by multiple senators. Additionally, a filibuster isn't necessarily a full stop anymore, either, now that rule changes have allowed other business to continue while the Senator(s) continue speaking. Not that it really matters, though, because for the last twenty years, the mere threat of a filibuster is usually enough to get the legislation dropped like a hot rock. (Which is extra silly, because none of these filibusters worked.)

2. ■ Strom Thurmond

Yep, it's yet another U.S. Senator. But hey, there's one more speech left on this list! You never know what could happen.

Strom Thurmond served as the Senator from South Carolina for nearly fifty years, and didn't even retire until he was 100 years old. To say he was obstinate would be an understatement on the scale of saying that our world-famous BML Burger (the BML stands for butter, mayo, and lard) is bad for you. (We prefer our catch phrase, "Apocalyptic to your health.")

In August of 1957, Thurmond broke the record for the longest solo filibuster in Senate history, a record that still stands to this day (crap, we just spoiled the fact that number one isn't a senator, didn't we?). At twenty-four hours and eighteen minutes, Senator Strom Thurmond talked for a freaking day straight without pausing. Reportedly, he even visited the Senate steam room (they have one of those?) for several hours beforehand in an attempt to extract as much water from his body as possible so he wouldn't need a pee break.

As for the bill Thurmond was protesting, well . . . it was the Civil Rights Act of 1957, which passed anyway. No one ever said he was a good guy. In fact, the other southern senators even got pissed at him for doing it because they'd all agreed *not* to filibuster the bill. Thurmond, like most "dixiecrats" (that is, southern Democrats) were opposed to federal desegregation and wanted to leave it up to the states, which would have meant we'd still have Whites Only signs in several states to this day, probably.

Amusingly, Thurmond's strong resistance to equal rights (he insisted he wasn't a racist until the day he died, to which we ask what course of action *would* have made him one in his mind) belied the fact that he had, and provided for, a secret mixed-race child with his family's black maid, a fact that didn't come out until after he died. That's historical drama movie villain stuff right there.

1. Lluis Colet and Jayasimha Ravirala

Boom! Not a U.S. Senator! Didn't see that coming, did you?

Ahem. Not only are Lluis Colet and Jayasimha Ravirala not U.S. politicians, they're not political figures at all. Well, not major ones, anyway. Unlike the rest of this list, Colet is a mere smalltime government employee in France and Ravirala is a former Indian Air Force member, and yet they have both held the Guinness World Record for the longest speech ever given. Specifically, Colet has held it *twice*.

The first time was in 2004, when he spoke for *forty-eight hours*. That's two whole days of yammering. We have great aunts who couldn't manage that.

That record was taken from him, though, by former military man turned public speaker Jayasimha Ravirala, who lectured for *120 hours* (that's five days if you're doing the math in your head right now) on "personality development concepts." Five freaking days on personality development. If it was us, we'd have simply walked to the podium, said, "Don't be an asshole," dropped the mic, and walked out. Three-second personality speech.

And yet, in 2009, Colet took the record back with a gobsmacking 124-hour speech. For perspective, that's only three hours less than it took for James Franco to get rescued in that movie where he cut off his arm. So what did Colet talk about for over five days? What any Frenchman talks about: Salvador Dali. Wait, that's not a stereotype, is it? Let's make it one, because we're terrible people. Wine, berets, striped shirts, and Salvador Dali. Anyway, Colet, who is of Catalan ancestry, spoke on Dali (a fellow Catalan), various aspects of Catalan history and culture, and even read from Catalan texts. Well, they say write what you know, and apparently that applies to speeches as well. (That's why we're following this book up with our self-help tome, *How to Be Really Awkward and Sometimes Just Freak Out for No Real Reason.*)

The **Five** Varieties of **Shortest Stories Ever Written**

In contemporary fiction, the trend is to keep stories short. People have got too much crap to do to sit around enjoying a good story or exploring the wonders of imagination. Seriously, who cares about enriching your life when your crops are wilting on Facebook? We mean that earnestly. We've poured too much time and effort into this stupid farm to just let it go.

Anyway, microfiction (an actual term) may seem like a relatively new thing, brought about by the invention of Twitter and texting, but it's actually a pretty solidly twentieth-century phenomenon. (Okay, that's still recent, relatively speaking, but you know what we mean.) The trend was essentially kick-started by someone (who was possibly one of America's most famous writers) at some unknown point in the last century (we'll get to all that).

Since then, it's practically become a writing institution, with authors all over the world trying to constrain themselves to minimalist word counts. As such, it's not really feasible (due to word counts, ironically) to try to list them all. Instead, we can separate them out by their respective word counts to make things a little easier on everyone. Cool? Cool.

One final note, our lawyers are super busy at the moment dealing with a thing (that we may or may not have caused, but don't worry, all the fires got put out before anyone *living* got hurt). As a result, we're going to err on the side of caution with regard to copyright, since reprinting these stories in their entirety (no matter how short they are) would still be a big no-no. If you're interested in reading these, Google 'em.

Oh, and as a thanks for buying this book, here's our free microbook as an exclusive bonus:

The Funniest Double-Entendre Sentence in the English Language: "Hey, lady, nice beaver!"

5. Fifty-Five Words

A story consisting of fifty-five words has, oddly, become a bit of a standard in the writing world. Derived from a writing challenge known as a "drabble," wherein two contestants write 100-word stories as quickly as possible (itself based on a Monty Python skit where a drabble is a word game where the first person to write a novel wins), the idea has since morphed into a fifty-five-word limit without the competitive aspect instead. (It's seen as a solo challenge, much like our attempts to eat those giant, pie-pan-sized burgers, which technically isn't really a challenge to us anymore, since we're all now capable of putting them away as a matter of rote.)

There are literally thousands of fifty-five-word stories, especially since the dawn of the Internet, where it's become a common prompt. Sites like 55 Words (*www.birdandmoon.com/55words*) and various blogging groups have massively popularized the format, so now basically anyone (including you, this crap isn't rocket science) can write a fifty-five-word story to call their own.

4. Seventeen Words

Okay, so seventeen-word stories aren't actually a thing, but there is one extremely popular one. Sort of. We'll explain.

It's commonly stated that the "shortest horror story ever written" goes like this: "The last man on Earth sat alone in a room. There was a knock on the door . . . " As far as horror stories go, it's not a bad one. But here's the thing—it really doesn't exist. Again, we'll explain.

The "story" was actually made up as part of the framing device for another story, Fredric Brown's "Knock." Brown takes the purported short story (which he, himself, made up) and decides to "add" to it (by coming up with a story about humans in an alien zoo or something. It's not really as clever as the first bit). It's sort of metafiction before metafiction was a big deal. Brown is taking this shortest horror story and adding his own twist on it, but technically he could write that it was a personified fart knocking at the door and it would still be the official version because he wrote it in the first place, dig?

To recap: Fredric Brown writes the "world's shortest horror story," but instead of being satisfied with that, creates a kind of legend around it, then publishes a story based on that story (which he wrote) and then, over the years, the legendary story ends up becoming way more popular than his "take" on the story, which may have been his intention all along.

And to add another twist, the shortest horror story part was vaguely based on a snippet in a book of odds and ends by early twentieth-century writer Thomas Bailey Aldrich, which was not quite so succinct, but covers the same bases, more or less. Still, Brown's version, while a paraphrase, is kind of its own thing, so he did essentially write it (without citing the original, the cur). But he still wrote it for another, larger piece. Now do you see why we say it doesn't exist? Well, good, maybe you can explain it to us sometime, mister. (Unlike Brown, we will totally acknowledge that that joke came from Daffy Duck.)

3. ■ Seven Words

Seven-word stories do exist as a common format, but they're not nearly as popular as fifty-five-word or six-word stories (which we'll get to shortly). Again, like seventeen-word stories, there is one standout that deserves to be mentioned.

In 1959, Guatemalan writer Augusto Monterroso wrote his most famous story, and one that's often said to be either the shortest story in the world (sadly untrue, since you can see that there are two more entries to go), the shortest story in Spanish (possibly true at one time, but probably not anymore), and the shortest historical fiction story ever written (could very well be).

Monterroso's story, titled "El Dinosaurio," is an epic journey through time, a precursor to one of the most popular movies of the '90s, or maybe neither of those. It consists of one sentence, describing a genderless narrator who awakens to find a dinosaur "still there," implying it was there when they fell asleep as well. That's really it. It doesn't sound like much, but it was a wildly popular story, and easily Monterroso's most famous outside of Guatemala. Who are we to argue with dinosaurs, after all?

In fact, Monterroso is one of the writers who helped kick off the microfiction phenomenon, but the lion's share of the credit goes to . . .

2. Six Words

Ernest Hemingway. *Maybe.* Let's back up. Sometime after Hemingway's death, this apocryphal story started creeping around (it has since become much more widespread since the Internet was hatched) that claimed that, on a bet, a young Ernest Hemingway contended that he could write an emotionally wrenching story in only six words. The result?

For sale: Baby shoes. Never worn.

Now, we're not saying it's not a really great piece, because it totally is. It takes a few seconds to snap into place and then you're just like . . . *whoa,* you know? It's, like, totally intense, bro. Or whatever. Anyway, the problem is that no one's ever proven that Hemingway really wrote it. Some of the earliest versions of the tale only date back to the 1990s, which has led many Hemingway researchers to conclude that it's just another tall tale about Hemingway's life.

Thing is, though, it kind of doesn't matter who wrote it anymore, because now it's become a phenomenon all its own. Six-word stories have become a hot property, even for established writers. In 2006, *Wired* magazine solicited dozens of six-word stories from huge names in the entertainment business, like Margaret Atwood, Neil Gaiman, Joss Whedon, Stan Lee, and even William

Shatner. Unsurprisingly, most of them are shockingly good. It turns out that you can do a lot more than you'd think in six words, which is probably why this format has taken off so quickly. But hey, if the six-word format is that awesome, what could you do with even shorter works?

1. ■ One Word

How do you write a one-word story? You can't really just have a story that's, like, "Gubernatorial," and that's it. Well, you could, but that would be kind of boring, wouldn't it?

The answer, of course, is titles. You can title a story whatever you want. People generally don't count that as part of the content of the story, right? So a more appropriate one-word story might be this:

"English Is a Marvelous Thing Because the First Two Syllables of a Single Word Relating to the Political Process Actually Sum Up That Process in and of Itself"

Gubernatorial.

There you go. A one-word comedy story, just for you. Don't say we never gave you nothin', kid. Okay, it's more of an essay than a story, but screw you, buddy. We're just working stiffs, here. We don't tell you your job.

This format still isn't as popular as six-word or fifty-five-word stories, but there is one notable entry, which is the *one letter* story. Sci-fi author Forrest J Ackerman wrote what is basically a one-of-a-kind story, titled "Cosmic Report Card: Earth." It's just one letter long, and we'll give you a huge spoiler: It's not a passing grade.

The story is, essentially, the history of humankind summed up extremely succinctly, at least in the opinion of Mr. Ackerman. (We'd argue that the invention of ice cream should bring us up to at least a D-, but what do we know?)

0. ■ Zero Words

Sorry, there is one more thing we should mention, which is the odd phenomenon of "zero word stories." How does that even work, you ask? Well, luckily, it's not anything too bizarre. They're stories made up of either only punctuation (no, not typographic genitals or anything like that, although that gives us an idea) or literally nothing at all.

Like the one-word story mentioned previously, these rely heavily on their titles. Two are written by sci-fi author Edward Wellen, "If Eve Had Failed to Conceive," which is a single punctuation mark (the one that normally comes at the end of a sentence), and "Why Booth Didn't Kill Lincoln," which is appropriately blank. (There's not exactly a grassy knoll in Lincoln's assassination.)

Another, written by Forrest J Ackerman (who wrote the one-letter story in the previous entry) and Daryl F. Mallett, is titled "A Typical Terran's Thought When Spoken to by an Alien from the Planet Quarn in Its Native Language," and it, too, is a single punctuation mark long. You can probably figure out which one. Also, note that it took *two* people to write that one. How do you think they split the workload?

The One-Word Poem That Really Pissed People Off

There's a really great way to make a lot of people very angry with just seven letters, and you don't have to shame your entire household in the process. Just ask poet Aram Saroyan, who, in 1965, wrote a one-word poem that managed to get even Congress furious.

The poem, typed hastily in the center of a sheet of paper before Saroyan went out on the town with a friend on an autumn night, is a single, misspelled word: "lighght." (If you're the kind of person who cares about what a poem "means": according to Saroyan, if it was just the word "light," you wouldn't notice it, and "lighghght" wouldn't have the same effect, but "lighght" makes you stop and look. It *illuminates* you, so to speak. You dig, man?)

Now, we've known some grammar Nazis in our time. We're betting some are reading this book right now. But a simple misspelled word shouldn't cause a shockwave that stretched all the way to the heart of the country, yet it did. The same year Saroyan composed *lighght*, the government began the National Endowment for the Arts, which gives grants and support to artists of all stripes.

Because Saroyan's poem was included in *The American Literary Anthology*, which had been given a grant by the NEA, he received a check for a cool $500 straight from Uncle Sam (meaning the U.S. tax-payers). Not bad for seven letters, right? That's almost $72 per character.

When fiscal conservatives in Washington, DC, found out, though, it caused an outrage. Not only was it "not a poem," it "wasn't even spelled right." The horror! Eventually, the controversy blew over and the NEA continued to operate, but even decades later, during the Reagan admin-istration, it was still trotted out as an example of wasteful government spending. And yet no one ever talks about the government grant we got to construct 700 bear suits, fill them with beef stew, and chuck them at moving cars. Although now we're thinking that wasn't the government, but just an old guy who kind of looked like Uncle Sam that dropped his wallet.

The Five Longest Words in English That Can Be Typed One-Handed

According to popular legend, the QWERTY style keyboard was invented not for speed, but artificial slowness, as typewriter keys might get stuck if the user typed too quickly. While that particular factoid is highly debatable, we can at least say that the standard keyboard layout has led to some interesting developments in the arena of wordplay.

(We're more inclined to buy the story that purports that the layout was designed so that the letters to spell "typewriter" would all appear in the top row, because otherwise that's just a super-eerie coincidence. Also, bonus fact: You can't spell any standard English words solely with the bottom row of keys on a keyboard because there are no vowels down there. And we bet you just went and checked.)

It turns out, there are several words, like "milk" and "fret," that can only be typed with one side of the keyboard, which is sort of awkward (but convenient if you're always holding a ham sandwich while typing, like we are). But surely those words must not be terribly common, and pure probability would state that they're not all that long, right? You're not wrong, imaginary reader, and don't call us surely. Wait, that joke doesn't work in print. Still, they aren't all that common and usually aren't extremely long. Except, you know, for the ones we're about to show you . . .

Left Hand

Ah, old lefty. That confusing monster of a hand (unless you're left-handed, of course). It does get the best vowels, even if righty gets more of them. We'll give lefty its time in the sun. (Before we use it to scratch our butts later. Eat it, lefty.)

5. **Extraverted** -adj. (*ecks-tra-ver-ted*), 11 letters

WHAT IT MEANS: An alternate spelling of extroverted, which means to be outgoing and friendly and cool, as opposed to introverted, which is to be quiet and shy and probably kind of boring. It's the high school cheerleader versus the cute, bookish girl with the glasses and the little smile when you catch her eye. (Also, there are actually lots of eleven-letter words that are lefty-only; we just picked this one as an example.)

A SAMPLE SENTENCE: "Despite his extraverted nature, even he wasn't quick to point out that the obvious solution to all of their problems was simply to find a genie, get three wishes, and to ask for everything to go back to the way it was before they tried to bring an ice cream monster to life."

4. **Aftereffects** -n. (*af-ter-eff-eckts*), 12 letters

WHAT IT MEANS: A delayed effect, like how the aftereffects of eating an entire bottle of Flintstones vitamins are that six hours later, you start to wonder if Fred was actually a real prehistoric guy that they based the show on, or something, man. And, like, do you think he really had a pet dinosaur? Oh, and did you know that Dino could talk in the early episodes? That's messed up, dude.

A SAMPLE SENTENCE: "Although the aftereffects wouldn't be apparent for many years yet, at the time the group decided it would be a fantastic idea to use their time machine to travel back to the 1940s and shave off half of Hitler's mustache."

What Is the Longest Place Name in the World?

What's the longest place name? You'd think it'd be a straightforward query, but there are two answers that have created an argument that's surprisingly far longer and even more bitter than the debate over whether or not *Napoleon Dynamite* is a good movie. The simple answer for both debates is this: It depends on who you ask.

Our first contender is eighty-five letters long, the Maori-named Taumatawhakatangihangakoauauotamateaturipukakapikimaungahoronukupokaiwhenuakitanatahu, a hill in New Zealand famous for having a ridiculous name and a Mountain Dew radio commercial made about its ridiculous name. Its official translation is, "The summit where Tamatea, the man with the big knees, the climber of mountains, the land-swallower who traveled about, played his nose flute to his loved one." Immediately, you learn two things about this particular area: That having big knees is a notable trait (our cleaning woman will be thrilled), and that some ladies dig the nose flute (ditto).

The second possibility is Bangkok, Thailand. Yeah, you heard us right. Only it's not actually called Bangkok in Thailand. Officially, it's Krungthepmahanakhon Amonrattanakosin Mahintharayutthaya Mahadilokphop Noppharatratchathaniburirom Udomratchaniwetmahasathan Amonphimanawatansathit Sakkathattiyawitsanukamprasit which, loosely translated, means, "City of angels, great city of immortals, magnificent city of the nine gems, seat of the king, city of royal palaces, home of gods incarnate, erected by Visvakarman at Indra's behest." At 169 letters, it's easily longer than New Zealand's hill.

Or is it? Bangkok's full name is purely ceremonial, and most Thai people don't even use it, preferring "Krung Thep," which simply means "City of Angels." (Bet you didn't know you had that in common with Thailand, Los Angeles.) In fact, there's a not insignificant percentage of Thai people who don't even *know* the whole thing, and since it's in an antiquated form of Thai, an even larger chunk don't even know what it means.

This gives rise to the argument that New Zealand's hill has a longer name, except most of their natives also give it a short name: Taumata. And since it's in Maori, only some New Zealanders actually understand what it means.

So really, it's whichever one has a stronger argument to you. We figure the only way to settle it for real is for them to undergo a series of stranger and more elaborate tests of skill, might, wisdom, and gastro-intestinal fortitude.

---

3. ■ *Desegregated* -adj. (*de-seg-re-gae-ted*), 12 letters

WHAT IT MEANS: To be without racial segregation. In case you've never paid attention to anything in your life until right now, once upon a time in America, it was considered okay to separate black and white people in various public institutions. This was discontinued in the twentieth century. Thus, desegregation.

A SAMPLE SENTENCE: "In the decades since the Civil Rights movement, desegregated schools and other progressive ideas have been put in place, and they are widely considered to be 'freaking awesome' by scholars."

2. ▪ Tesseradecades -n. (*tess-er-a-deck-ades*), 14 letters

WHAT IT MEANS: The plural of tesseradecade, which is to be arranged into groups of fourteen. So one is solo, two is a duo, three is a trio, and fourteen is a tesseradecade. Presumably there are other things in between those, but hell if we know what they are. It's not even a very useful term, since there aren't any major sports that have fourteen players or anything like that. (Except Quidditch. Yes, there are only seven players on a Quidditch team, we know . . . but that makes for a tesseradecade of players on the pitch at one time. Ha!)

A SAMPLE SENTENCE: "They split us into tesseradecades and showed us each a film that informed us that the other groups were plotting against us, and that we should report any unpatriotic statements we heard while interacting with them."

1. ▪ Aftercataracts -n. (*aff-ter-cat-uh-rackts*), 14 letters

WHAT IT MEANS: The plural of aftercataract, which is a condition where, after a particular cataract surgery where the eye's clouded-over lens has been removed and replaced with an artificial lens, the replacement eye lens will sometimes (as in very rarely) once again cloud up. It's also sometimes referred to as a "secondary cataract," but that takes two hands to type. Luckily, an aftercataract is usually even easier to correct than the original cataract with a simple laser procedure.

A SAMPLE SENTENCE: "As luck would have it, the procedure to remove the aftercataracts from my eyes also gave me superhuman X-ray vision, and you're almost out of milk in your fridge."

Right Hand

Righty, you old stalwart. We believe in you. (You know the word "sinister" comes from the Latin word *sinestra*, which means left-handed?)

5. Lollipop -n. (*law-lee-pop*), 8 letters

WHAT IT MEANS: Well, we probably don't have to explain what a lollipop (lollypop also works) is for you, so we'll just share some trivia about a famous lollipop—the one presented to Dorothy by the Lollipop Guild in *The Wizard of Oz*. The actor who played that Munchkin is named Jerry Maren, and he's the oldest surviving male Munchkin actor from the film. Added coolness: He helped found the Little People of America, the preeminent organization for those affected with dwarfism in the United States.

A SAMPLE SENTENCE: "Sometimes a man has a dream, and nothing can stop that dream, and that's why I have to follow my destiny, which is to be the inventor of the ham-and-cheese-flavored lollipop."

4. Honolulu -n. (*hawn-o-loo-loo*), 8 letters

WHAT IT MEANS: The capital of Hawaii, the fiftieth state of the United States of America, but in the Hawaiian language itself it means "place of shelter," so when the Rolling Stones were doing "Gimme Shelter," we really should have just pointed to Honolulu and said, "Have at it, fellas. Keith, it's 1969 and that means you're still made of drugs at this point, so you might get stuck in customs for a while."

A SAMPLE SENTENCE: "I had always wanted to visit Honolulu, but upon arriving, I noticed a distinct lack of palm trees and sand, which led me to seek out the tourist information desk, and it was only then that I realized I wasn't in Honolulu, but Hawnaloo, Michigan."

3. Homophony -n. (*hawm-off-oh-nee*), 9 letters

WHAT IT MEANS: The state of being homophonic, which is not something you call a bigoted person. If you'll recall from middle school English, words that are homophonic sound the same, but mean different things, like "in" and "inn." It also applies to music, in which multiple parts moving in harmony create chords. If that doesn't mean anything to you, just trust us: it generally sounds nice.

A SAMPLE SENTENCE: "The homophony of their voices created a stirring sound not unlike that of a giant loosening his bowels upon a stone ravine in a thunderstorm, which is to say that it was really, very terrible."

2. Monimolimnion -n. (*mon-ih-mo-lim-ne-on*), 13 letters

WHAT IT MEANS: The lowest layer of water in a meromictic lake. Much like your bathtub, most lakes experience a mixing of the waters at the bottom and top layers, sometimes multiple times a year (depending on how much you bathe . . . wait, this metaphor got weird). This is known as a holomictic lake. In meromictic lakes, however, the deep waters and surface waters never mix, creating two or more distinct layers to the lake, like if you mix water and oil. Typically, the monimolimnion is highly oxygen deprived, leaving it uninhabitable to most aquatic life.

Also interesting: Sometimes CO_2 can build up in the monimolimnion, and if something forces the waters to mix (like, say, an earthquake), it can cause a massive cloud of poisonous gases (called a limnic eruption). It's cool science, but also very deadly, as two in recent history have killed thousands in Cameroon.

A SAMPLE SENTENCE: "In what appears to be a first, scientists have announced that the monimolimnion of a local lake has been found to contain a naturally growing form of delicious taffy, but they are cautioning residents not to go diving for it until they're done eating it."

1. ■ Johnny-jump-up -n. (*jon-nee-jump-up*), 14 characters

WHAT IT MEANS: A colloquial name for a flower formally known as the viola tricolor. It's also called numerous other names, like heartsease and wild pansy. Basically, it's a really nice purple and yellow flower that blossoms perennially. Now, if you wanna get real technical, there's only twelve letters up there, but the hyphen's still a keystroke, so we'll give it a pass. Also, that means lefty has two fourteen letter words and righty just gets a technical one. You win this time, lefty. Now, let's shake on it and all go home.

A SAMPLE SENTENCE: "I awoke in a small patch of johnny-jump-up with no clothes, no idea where I was, and no memory of where I had been the night before."

Twenty
of the
Longest Words
Without A, E, I, O, or U

In English, we have the five standard vowels, but then we have that crazy *Y*, too. Who do you think you are, *Y*, with your ability to be used as both a vowel and a consonant? Make up your mind, because you're seriously bumming us out.

So we end up with those words like "sky" and "shy," which are pretty short and we can just accept them and move on. But then we get to the ones like these, where the madness of *Y* just doesn't seem to end (and some that form entirely new insanities which we've never seen before). Let us introduce you to . . .

20. Cwm -n. (*coom*)

WHAT IT MEANS: Yeah, remember how we mentioned new insanities? This is one of them. As it happens, Welsh has yet another vowel in the form of w that they can toss into words, and we've picked a few of them up in English. A cwm is a small, bowl-shaped basin carved into a mountain over centuries by a glacier. Now you can screw with people when you play it in Scrabble.

A SAMPLE SENTENCE: "The cwm at the top of the mountain holds the greatest secret ever sought by mankind, which is the method to get cats to listen to you when you tell them not to do stuff."

19. Nth -n. (*enth*)

WHAT IT MEANS: It's a mathematical term for the variable *n*. It can also be used in the exponential form, so 6^n would be six to the *n*th power, which is also useful for insults, so you can tell someone they're an asshole to the *n*th degree.

A SAMPLE SENTENCE: "The formula was so complex that the *n*th position was taken up by a collection of nuns arranged into the shape of the letter *n*."

18. Pht -int. (*pft*)

WHAT IT MEANS: A sound made out of exasperation, typically followed by that lewd fake masturbating gesture in contemporary usage. It can also be spelled as "pfft," "phpht," and "omg, are you freaking serious right now?"

A SAMPLE SENTENCE: "'Pht, come on, like Luke and Leia won't end up together with Han out of the picture, they're practically made for each other,' I said as we walked out of *The Empire Strikes Back*."

17. Brr -int. (*burr*)

WHAT IT MEANS: What you say after walking outside without a coat in the middle of winter. After all the swear words, that is. Brr (or brrr or brrrr, etc.) are onomatopoeic interjections for being cold, and yeah, they're totally in the dictionary.

A SAMPLE SENTENCE: "Do you ever think walruses get too cold and are all like, 'Brr, I made a wrong turn at that last glacier'?"

16. Hmm -int. (*humm*)

WHAT IT MEANS: A thoughtful sound we sometimes make, even unconsciously. Basically, you're putting on your thinking deerstalker cap (everyone has one of those, right?) and trying to puzzle out the mysteries of the universe. Or you're trying to decide what you want from the menu at the taco stand. Whichever.

A SAMPLE SENTENCE: "'Hmm,' he said to his cat as he arranged the matchsticks into tiny stick figures and then lit them each on fire, 'do you think I should wear pants today?'"

15. **Shh** -int. (*sh*)

WHAT IT MEANS: Be quiet! (As in, "We're trying to watch the freaking movie, so *be quiet!*")

A SAMPLE SENTENCE: "Shh, this is a library," the woman told us, in hopes that we would take our beatboxing session outside.

14. **Psst** -int. (*pst*)

WHAT IT MEANS: It's the universal language for, "Hey, buddy, where can a guy get rubber sealant, a pair of pantyhose, and a lizard at this time of night?" Or that's what we always assume is going to happen when people *psst* at us, anyway.

A SAMPLE SENTENCE: "'Psst,' said the stranger, who did not wait for acknowledgement but continued, 'Do you think it's a better idea to buy marital aids in bulk, or just one at a time?'"

13. **Crwth** -n. (*crooth*)

WHAT IT MEANS: Obviously, this is another Welsh loanword. You'd think we'd just refuse to take them, but in this case, we have to. A crwth is a Welsh instrument, and since they invented it, we just have to go with it, we guess. It's a stringed instrument, sort of like a lyre, except it's played with a bow. It sounds a little like a bowed dulcimer, but if you're not from rural Appalachian country you probably have no idea what that sounds like anyway. Go YouTube it.

A SAMPLE SENTENCE: "I had heard horror stories about airlines and guitars, but I never once considered that they'd somehow be able to transport my crwth into an alternate dimension where it is now king in a land with no vowels."

12. ■ Cwtch -n. (*cootch*)

WHAT IT MEANS: Yes, it's really pronounced that way. Calm down, all of you who have the giggles right now. Essentially, a cwtch is a hidey-hole for important stuff. So if you have something you'd like to keep all to yourself, well, you can just jam it straight in your cwtch. It can also mean a hug, so if there's someone dear to you that you'd like to show your appreciation, give 'em a little cwtch. They'll be glad for it.

A SAMPLE SENTENCE: "I had the painter over last week, and when he was working in the bedroom he ended up putting his whole foot right in my cwtch, because it turned out that the boards underneath my closet floor were rotted through."

11. ■ Syzygy -n. (*siz-idg-ee*)

WHAT IT MEANS: Now here's a word that's worth its weight in Scrabble points. However much those weigh. (Also, just so we're on the level with you, there are a whole lot of other words that only have *Y* as a vowel, and there's no way we're including all of them; we just picked the fun ones.)

Anyway, there's not just one definition of syzygy because every discipline of science ever has picked it up and used it for something. Essentially, it means two (or more) things that are inextricably tied together, like conjoined twins, but not as heartbreaking and stuff. The most common use is in astronomy, where it refers to three celestial objects aligned so that they're in a straight row, like the alignment that will end our world in 2453 according to the hobo behind our office building.

A SAMPLE SENTENCE: "The syzygy behind chocolate and peanut butter has become so linked in human consciousness that if one were to now exist without the other, reality itself would bend and create distortion in the form of hallucinations that resemble racecar beds."

10. ■ Styryl -n. (*stie-rill*)

WHAT IT MEANS: A chemical derived from styrene, which is a part of polystyrene, a type of plastic. So basically, it's a weird second cousin of plastic, and maybe they met once at a family reunion when they were kids or something. It's also called cinnamyl, which makes it sound like a delicious breakfast pastry of some variety. (Please don't try to eat it.)

A SAMPLE SENTENCE: "With a sock filled with empty water balloons, two dozen cheeseburgers stacked neatly into a pile, a cougar that can bark like a dog, and a vial of styryl, you'd be surprised what a man can get up to in this day and age."

9. ■ Schwyz -n. (*schveets*)

WHAT IT MEANS: A town (also a canton, which is a bit like a state) in Switzerland. The original name, Suittes, is vaguely derived from the Old High German (an archaic form of modern German) word *suedan*, which means "to burn," since they burned the forest in the area to build the original village. So it basically means "Burn Town," or something like that. Until we resurrect this old German ancestor of a guy we met on Craigslist, we won't know for sure.

A SAMPLE SENTENCE: "We were happy then, visiting Europe, but our favorite place of all was Schwyz, because it was the last place we visited before the demon spirit that lives in those old bones came into our lives and made us miserable."

8. Phytyl -n. (*fie-till*)

WHAT IT MEANS: A chemical derivative of phytol, a compound that comes from digested chlorophyll. Basically, it works like this: Cows (and other animals that chew cud) eat greens, which breaks down the chlorophyll and creates phytol, among numerous other chemicals. The animals absorb that phytol as phytanic acid, and we get that when we eat products derived from those animals. Boom. Science. Phytyl isn't used directly in anything, but is usually combined with other chemicals (such as acetate) for various lab purposes.

A SAMPLE SENTENCE: "Adding phytyl to the mixture had some unintended consequences, and I don't know if Wilhelm and his dog will ever be the same . . . and by that I mean different again, because now they're literally the same being."

7. Glycyl -n. (*gly-sill*)

WHAT IT MEANS: This is the last organic chemistry term, we swear. Glycyl is a derivative of glycine, an amino acid that happens to have a lot of commercial uses as well. For people food, it's often used as a sweetener (not related to glucose). It's also employed in cosmetics, toiletries, medicines, and probably in the back of a shoe store somewhere as well, for all the other work it does.

A SAMPLE SENTENCE: "The last thing my father ever told me was, 'Son, you're going to find out something that I wish I had known when I was your age, and it's that glycyl is not for styling your manhood hair; anyone who tells you that is just trying to win a bet.'"

6. **Sphynx** -n. (*sfinks*)

WHAT IT MEANS: Not to be confused with the Sphinx, a giant, noseless statue found in Egypt. These are a weird breed of hairless cats that makes our bathing suit areas itch just looking at them. Not to say they aren't probably super lovable, but come on, they look like an old guy's business hanging out of the bottom of his shorts. They're so . . . wrinkly.

A SAMPLE SENTENCE: "The Sphynx coiled its hairless tail around the gun, sliding the tip easily through the trigger guard, and pointed it at me in one swift motion saying, 'Now that you have discovered the secret cat plans to destroy humanity, I'm afraid I'm going to have to kill you and then bury you by kicking litter over you.'"

5. **Cywydd** -n. (*cuh-with*)

WHAT IT MEANS: Another strange Welsh word. This one refers to a certain type of verse found in Welsh poetry (and we can't even imagine what that sounds like), where lines are written as harmonious rhyming couplets. Fun fact: The Welsh also have their own word for harmony, and that's *cynghanedd*. Is this whole language just made up of Cthulhu speak, or what?

A SAMPLE SENTENCE: "The poem, which appeared to be a simple eulogy written in cywydd, was actually the password to a small underground club on the north side of Cardiff, where people entered all the time, but never seemed to come back out."

4. ■ Tsktsks -v. (*tisk-tisks*)

WHAT IT MEANS: Chances are you've heard it from your grandma at some point. When someone tsktsks you, that means exactly what it sounds like: they've made that disapproving "tsk tsk" sound at you. You know the one. We don't know about you, but we hear it in our heads pretty much constantly nowadays.

A SAMPLE SENTENCE: "The leprechaun looks me up and down and tsktsks, 'Not a spot of gold on you, but you'd better jump into this boiling cauldron so we can check your bones and make sure.'"

3. ■ Lytdybr -n. (*leeyit-deeb-ur*)

WHAT IT MEANS: Lytdybr is actually a fairly new word, as in it was invented this century. It's a Russian-English slang word that essentially means "a trivial blog post." It technically belongs to both languages simply because of the weird way it came to be. In Russian, the word "diary" is spelled *дневник* (dnevnik), but because bilingual Russian-English writers will sometimes forget to change their keyboard layout from English to Cyrillic and vice versa, some unknown person(s) accidentally typed "lytdybr" (the same keystrokes as *дневник* on a QWERTY keyboard layout) when referring to their blog(s). After a time, the typo went viral and took on its own, more specialized meaning of a lame or boring blog post, where it's since been picked up by English-speaking people as well. It's even been transliterated back into Russian as *лытдыбр* (pronounced more or less the same).

A SAMPLE SENTENCE: "I wrote a total lytdybr today because I just didn't have anything going on besides the giant, steel pyramid that came down from space and is now hovering above my house, casting ominous beams of light, and making weird sounds—but no one wants to hear about that."

2. **Symphysy** -n. (*sim-fis-see*)

WHAT IT MEANS: An old-fashioned spelling of symphysis, which itself is a medical term that refers to structures in the human body (usually bones) that are fused together, like several of the bones in the sternum and hip, for example. Technically, it could be used outside of medicine, but it's still meant to refer to something organic, like, say, a genetically intertwined badger and goat in your garage. (Deadly like a badger, screams like a goat.)

A SAMPLE SENTENCE: "The symphysy of the pelvic bone to the spine was something I hoped to reinforce, essentially turning my spinal cord into a giant extension of my penis."

1. **Twyndyllyngs** -n. (*twin-dil-ling*)

WHAT IT MEANS: A Welsh (of course!) spelling of "twinling," a very archaic word meaning twin. Even worse, the Middle English form of twinling was "twynlynge." It's pretty lucky that we've pared that one down over the centuries, because the Minnesota Twins already have enough problems as it is. (Sorry, Minnesotans.)

A SAMPLE SENTENCE: "Days before the birth, all the horses in the village died, a dead tree's branches formed an arcane symbol on the ground, the moon was red for three nights in a row, and the town drunk's dog began to bark backward, but the twyndyllyngs were so cute that we decided it was all just a big coincidence."

The Five Longest Names in the World

Did you ever feel bad for that kid in your class whose name was Zachariah Wittgenstein Johannesburg because he constantly had to spell it out for people? Or, even worse, maybe *you* were poor old Zach J., who probably curses his parents every day and has half-completed a name change form a dozen times, but can't bring himself to actually finish it.

Our name is, essentially, who we are in the world. It's one of the main ways we distinguish ourselves from one another (besides flamboyant hair styles, forehead tattoos, and other things like that). Several ancient cultures believed names held power, and if that's true, these people are probably the most badass mofos on the planet.

Get ready to be glad you never had to call these names out loud.

5. Rosalind Arusha Arkadina Altalune Florence Thurman-Busson

You probably knew someone growing up who had two middle names, but Uma Thurman's kid has them beat. Baby Luna (her parents' nickname for her, presumably from the Altalune part) has got five of them, and her mom is awesome to boot.

Born in July 2012 to *Pulp Fiction* and *Kill Bill* actress Thurman and her husband, financier Arpad Busson, the couple waited three months to reveal her name to the public, which is probably a pretty appropriate length of time with a name like that. While she's only fifth on this list, Luna does have the great distinction of having the longest celebrity baby name in the world. And come on, it's no weirder than Moon Unit or Apple.

4. ■ Captain Fantastic

Englishman George Garratt, who obviously did not have enough things to do at the age of nineteen, changed his name to "Captain Fantastic Faster Than Superman Spiderman Batman Wolverine Hulk And The Flash Combined" in 2008. Reportedly, he did it completely on a whim through an online service that helped facilitate name changes. Amazingly, the government (and the superheroes whose names he totally jacked) accepted it, and he's been Captain Fantastic ever since.

One quibble we have, though: Wolverine isn't really known for being fast, is he? Superman can fly and is faster than a speeding bullet; Spider-Man (yes, there's a hyphen there) can web sling, which you better believe is a very fast way to get around NYC; Batman can soar a bit and he has the Batmobile, which is probably pretty damn fast; The Hulk can jump several miles in a single bound, so his running speed's gotta be something crazy; and, of course, The Flash is The Flash. Duh. He's fast.

But Wolverine's just a short Canadian dude with a tank inside his body, basically. Sure, he doesn't get tired easily, but that's stamina, not speed. And yes, Captain Fantastic claims to be faster than all of them combined, but Wolverine's a bit of an outlier, isn't he? You might as well say you're faster than the postman or something.

Yes, we just nitpicked and nerded out over a guy's made-up name. Wanna fight about it?

3. ■ Barnaby Marmaduke Usanky

Scottish artist Nick Usanky got bored of his regular name and decided to go for something more exotic. Way exotic, apparently, because he decided to not only change his name to Barnaby Marmaduke (we sincerely hope that's not a reference to the cartoon dog), but also gave himself a middle name for each letter of the alphabet, because why not.

His full name is now Barnaby Marmaduke Aloysius Benjy Cobweb Dartagnan Egbert Felix Gaspar Humbert Ignatius Jayden Kasper Leroy Maximilian Neddy Obiajulu Pepin Quilliam Rosencrantz Sexton Teddy Upwood Vivatma Wayland Xylon Yardley Zachary Usanky.

Reportedly, his friends and family have so far refused to call him Barnaby. Imagine that. Luckily, they've got twenty-seven other names to call him, some of which are fairly common, like Zachary and Jayden. According to Usanky, each of the names represents a special memory, so we're wondering what the story is behind some of these, like Sexton and Xylon. In theory, it's probably not a bad thing to have your life story encoded in your name. In practice, it's terrible to write on tax forms. "Full name" must bring on enormous feelings of dread.

2. Hubert Blaine Wolfe+585, Sr.

Mr. Wolfe+585, a German-born typesetter from Philadelphia, is one of only two people on this list who was (maybe) actually born with his insane name (the other being Uma Thurman's little girl). So, you know, he can (maybe) thank his parents for giving him a name so crazy that he has to put "+585" at the end of his name to represent the 585 remaining letters in his surname. He can also thank them for giving him one name for each letter of the alphabet, much like Barnaby Usanky chose to do to himself above.

We're going to refer to him as Mr. Wolfe+585 or Hubert (his chosen first name, probably from a hat) because his full name is so long it's going to give our editors fits, but here goes anyway:

Adolph Blaine Charles David Earl Frederick Gerald Hubert Irvin John Kenneth Lloyd Martin Nero Oliver Paul Quincy Randolph Sherman Thomas Uncas Victor William Xerxes Yancy Zeus Wolfeschlegelsteinhausenbergerdorffvoralternwarengewissenhaftschaferswessenschafewarenwohlgepflegeundsorgfaltigkeitbeschutzenvonangreifendurchihrraubgierigfeindewelchevoralternzwolftausendjahresvorandieerscheinenwanderersteerdemenschderraumschiffgebrauchlichtalsseinursprungvonkraftgestartseinlangefahrthinzwischensternartigraumaufdersuchenachdiesternwelchegehabtbewohnbarplanetenkreisedrehensichundwohinderneurassevonverstandigmenschlichkeitkonntefortplanzenundsicherfreuenanlebenslanglichfreudeundruhemitnichteinfurchtvorangreifenvonandererintelligentgeschopfsvonhinzwischensternartigraum, Senior.

Feel better? We sure do. Yes, that's a real last name. Sort of. According to several sources who have researched this over the years, Mr. Wolfe+585 does exist and does report it as his real name (he has also gone by Wolfeschlegelsteinhausenbergerdorff, which *is* a regular German surname, and Wolfeschlegelsteinhausenbergerdorffvoralternwarengewissenhaftschaferswessenschaftswarenwohlgefutternundsorgfaltigkeitbeschutzenvorangreifendurchihrraubgierigfiends, which we'll come back to).

It's possible that his parents were some sort of jokesters who planned this whole thing out. It's worth noting, however, that the German used in the name is pretty crappy, and was probably not picked by a native German-speaker (it also has a bunch of weird references to aliens). Our best guess? Someone at Guinness World Records, who originally printed the "full version," thought they'd have a little fun with Hubert Wolfeschlegelsteinhausenbergerdorff's already long name and it stuck, so he went and had it legally changed to that. In fact, after a few years, even Guinness just reported it as Wolfeschlegelsteinhausenbergerdorff before dropping the category entirely in the '80s.

Our second best guess is that he really does have a much longer surname: The aforementioned Wolfeschlegelsteinhausenbergerdorffvoralternwarengewissenhaftschaferswessenschaftswarenwohlgefutternundsorgfaltigkeitbeschutzenvorangreifendurchihrraubgierigfiends, which is what he said was "on the envelope" at his birth in one interview. That name, while supremely long, has no mention of aliens whatsoever, and actually refers to a family of shepherds protecting their flock from wolves using slings, according to our German translator, Evan. That's *way* more likely to be an actual German family name, albeit a crazy and ridiculously long one that might require being shortened upon moving to America and/or playing up for curious people.

Or his last name is actually Hitler, and he figured anything was better than that.

1. Red Dreams

When Dawn McManus's son, Kyle, passed away at the age of sixteen in 2007, she vowed to start a charity that would help kids engage in the arts and creativity in all its forms, just like Kyle had loved to do. It's an adorable story and gesture, and it's even sweeter that the McManus family held a 2012 fundraiser for their charity, Red Dreams, and if the fundraiser met its goal, Dawn McManus promised to change her actual name to Red Dreams.

They did, and she did, but if that wasn't heartwarming enough, she decided to take things a step further by adding 159 middle names—the names of each of the children her charity had helped at that point. She ended up inadvertently claiming the world record for the longest name for a person.

The full name is a mouthful, but it's also way cute that she did it. Ready for the whole thing? Okay, here we go (sorry once again, editors!): Red Wacky League Antlez Broke the Stereo Neon Tide Bring Back Honesty Coalition

Feedback Hand of Aces Keep Going Captain Let's Pretend Lost State of Dance Paper Taxis Lunar Road Up Down Strange All and I Neon Sheep Eve Hornby Faye Bradley AJ Wilde Michael Rice Dion Watts Matthew Appleyard John Ashurst Lauren Swales Zoe Angus Jaspreet Singh Emma Matthews Nicola Brown Leanne Pickering Victoria Davies Rachel Burnside Gil Parker Freya Watson Alisha Watts James Pearson Jacob Sotheran Darley Beth Lowery Jasmine Hewitt Chloe Gibson Molly Farquhar Lewis Murphy Abbie Coulson Nick Davies Harvey Parker Kyran Williamson Michael Anderson Bethany Murray Sophie Hamilton Amy Wilkins Emma Simpson Liam Wales Jacob Bartram Alex Hooks Rebecca Miller Caitlin Miller Sean McCloskey Dominic Parker Abbey Sharpe Elena Larkin Rebecca Simpson Nick Dixon Abbie Farrelly Liam Grieves Casey Smith Liam Downing Ben Wignall Elizabeth Hann Danielle Walker Lauren Glen James Johnson Ben Ervine Kate Burton James Hudson Daniel Mayes Matthew Kitching Josh Bennett Evolution Dreams.

Yeah, it's silly and a bit of a publicity stunt, but at least she's not wiping her butt with the money or anything. It's going to kids and helping them learn to make movies and become photographers and awesome stuff like that, which means they're not sitting at home playing video games on the couch, which is what most of our generation did, and look at all of us now. Handsome and talented and also billionaire geniuses, except pretty much the opposite of those things.

The Two Longest English Surnames

Want an instant and easy way to make sure no one ever forgets you? Just change your name to one of these last names, which are the longest in the English language. By the time people figure out how to pronounce them, they'll always lovingly stash you away in long-term memory as "that asshole with the ridiculous name."

First, there's the long and storied British family name of Fetherston-haugh. Before you pop a blood vessel trying to pronounce it, the correct way is "fenshaw." There hasn't been a bigger waste of letters since Dan Brown wrote that sequel to *The Da Vinci Code*. Also, we're not even sure the letters are in the right order for that pronunciation, but our vision starts to double and we hear distant bells tolling when we look at it, so sure, whatever.

It's not a silly, made-up name either. There have been two Fetherstonhaugh Baronets (a step under a Baron) in the eighteenth century, a twentieth-century politician, a Canadian architect, and a cricket player (because of course there's a cricket player with that name) that can be counted as famous Fetherstonhaughs.

The second surname is MacGhilleseatheanaich, which is pronounced something like the noise you'd make gargling vegetable oil. Our actually Irish friend Gary says it's something like "ma-gill-seth-en-ack," but even he's not certain, so we're just going to assume the real pronunciation can kill someone.

Technically, MacGhilleseatheanaich is a Gaelic name, but that's close enough to English that we'll count it. (Please don't hurt us, Irish militant groups.)

While there aren't many famous people with the name MacGhilleseatheanaich, it's not a made-up name either. It's not a particularly common one, but it's not some punchline to an Irish stereotype joke, either. Speaking of, did you hear the one about the Irishman who confused his whiskey with leprechaun pee?

Hey, wow. Where did all those flaming bottles flying toward our office windows come from?

Ten of the Craziest Auto-Antonyms in the English Language

Auto-antonyms are words that have the unique property of meaning one thing and its exact opposite simultaneously. It's like a cat that can't make up its mind if it wants to eat or go poop first. Wait, that's a horrible metaphor. Forget we said that.

You probably never even think about it. Dust, for example, can mean to remove fine particulates (like when dusting), but it can also mean to add them (like dusting a cake with sugar). We're also getting there with literally, which now means both in reality and figuratively at the same time. (If that annoys you, you literally need better hobbies.) The following are words you probably hear every day that you likely never even considered contradictory before now. Warning: This list might make you a little crazy and incapable of ever thinking about these words the same way again.

10. Bolt

FIRST MEANING: To secure or fasten in place; usually with, you know, a bolt. If you don't want someone to take stuff, you bolt it down. You securely bolt car parts back into place after you're done . . . doing whatever it is you do with them. We're not car people.

SECOND MEANING: To run quickly and get the hell out of there. If you're TPing your high school teacher's house, you totally bolt when the fuzz shows up.

So you have staying in place and not staying in place in the same word. Interesting! (That will come up again later.)

AN AMBIGUOUS SENTENCE: "He bolted it, a bit too late, when he heard the screen door crash against its frame."

Bill

FIRST MEANING: A bill of currency. Legal tender. Dolla dolla bills, y'all.

SECOND MEANING: An invoice or order of sale. Those things you hate seeing your mailbox (or e-mail inbox if you're with the times, grandpa).

So, y'know, you pay your bills with bills. You can bill those bills and they're gone, you dig?

AN AMBIGUOUS SENTENCE: "Now that we've got all these bills, this month's budget is going to look a lot different."

Cleave

FIRST MEANING: A separation, like cleaving meat or a woman's fancy cleavage. Basically, to bring two things apart. Like boobs.

SECOND MEANING: To cling or stick to. A tight dress cleaves to you, and if someone challenges you because you still think Tom Cruise is a good actor even if he is a complete weirdo, you cleave to your beliefs.

So cleaving is both holding tight and separating, perhaps with a seatbelt or handbag strap.

AN AMBIGUOUS SENTENCE: "Whenever she felt unsure about something, her instincts would tell her to cleave it harder than ever before."

7. Buckle

FIRST MEANING: To close or fasten, like buckling your seatbelt or regular belt.

SECOND MEANING: To come apart or collapse, like when a chair buckles under you and you know it's time to lay off your new Pop-Tart diet.

Therefore, buckling is both holding fast and totally coming to pieces. If you don't buckle in your gut, the fly on your pants might buckle.

AN AMBIGUOUS SENTENCE: "As he struggled to bring the two halves together, they finally, and terribly, buckled under his fingers."

6. Fine

FIRST MEANING: Acceptable, good enough. Much to George Carlin's chagrin, most people's days are just fine.

SECOND MEANING: Very nice, pleasing. That gentleman is very fine looking in his gym socks and nothing else.

Thus, fine means both "eh" (coupled with that back-and-forth hand wave) and "this crack cocaine sure is fine, may I have some more?"

AN AMBIGUOUS SENTENCE: "I won the lottery, got hit by a car, met the woman of my dreams, and burned my house to the ground, so I guess you could say today was fine."

5. Oversight

FIRST MEANING: To watch over or supervise. Optimus Prime had oversight of the Autobots, much like George Washington was given oversight of the Continental Army (yeah, we went for Transformers first, sorry).

SECOND MEANING: To make a mistake or error. An oversight led to Brad Pitt's legal name actually being Magilla Gorilla at birth. (Note to Brad Pitt's lawyers: That is untrue and we're just trying to be funny).

In theory, with proper oversight, oversights would not happen, but an oversight in someone's oversight can lead to further oversight oversights.

AN AMBIGUOUS SENTENCE: "Due to your horrible oversight, the entire project has become, as my dear, sweet old grandmother would have put it, 'a total, unabashed f**ked-up horsed**ked s**tstorm,' because she was a woman who had a way with words."

4. Custom

FIRST MEANING: An ordinary practice. In some restaurants, it is the regular custom to have all patrons remove their pants. It isn't like that anywhere, ever? New restaurant idea, everyone! What's a health code violation?

SECOND MEANING: Something intended for a specialized purpose. A custom dye job that makes your back hair look like racing stripes, for example.

Custom means both general and specific. Let's start a custom custom of customizing our customs to suit our needs, which usually involves having strangers remove their pants.

AN AMBIGUOUS SENTENCE: "This custom . . . whatever you call it, is dangerous and potentially lethal if used in certain third world countries."

3. Clip

FIRST MEANING: To cut or trim. Get your hair clipped at Donald Trump's barber and you'll never need to worry about your hair again. (Because he's good. We're not insinuating that Donald Trump is secretly bald or has some weird hairpiece. That would be ridiculous and irresponsible of us.)

SECOND MEANING: To attach or affix. Y'know, like a paperclip or a chip clip or one of those alligator clips that you can fold around and make look like AT-ATs.

So clip is to remove and to attach, which is probably really confusing for electricians who tell their apprentices to clip a cord that's in their way.

AN AMBIGUOUS SENTENCE: "Are you completely sure you want all that hair clipped *down there*?"

2. Original

FIRST MEANING: Plain or standard. Original Recipe chicken at KFC happens to be the best chicken they make, but that's merely a coincidence.

SECOND MEANING: Completely new or underived. An original art piece might be priceless while a cover band's original tunes are probably pretty worthless.

Original means both old-fashioned and new simultaneously, which is good, because we were looking for just the right adjective for our one-person theatre show, *I Was a Teenage Diarrhea Victim*.

AN AMBIGUOUS SENTENCE: "'This isn't original,' she said, staring at the robot camels and zombie horses that gazed up at her."

1. ■ Fast

FIRST MEANING: Speedy or quick, like that dearest American love affair, fast food. After all, what is life for if not paying someone else to make your food in about five minutes?

SECOND MEANING: Firmly or tightly. Stuck fast, held fast, break fast. Wait, not that last one. We're just really hungry after talking about fast food.

Thus, fast means both to move with rapidity and to not move at all. What if instead of being really fast, The Flash was really *fast*, like his legs were made of glue? Instead of The Flash, he could be That Guy Who Never Moves. Come on, it's not the worst idea in comics. Probably.

AN AMBIGUOUS SENTENCE: "He was so fast, his feet were skinned and bloody by the time he went to bed that night."

The Six Longest Song Titles Ever

Who doesn't love a long song? The kind that go on for thirty minutes or more, you know? Everyone who's ever listened to the radio before, that's who. Luckily, in recent decades, songs have trended toward shorter runtimes. No more epic twenty-minute guitar solos, except in extremely niche music genres, and that seems to be the way people prefer it.

Here's what has gotten longer, though: Song titles. Have you looked at the back of a Fall Out Boy CD? The tracklist is longer than the credits, most of the time. We assume they're only doing it to screw with radio DJs.

We're not just being old-timers and complaining about how music was better back in our day (back in our day, the popular stuff was just as terrible as it is now). We're just saying, long song titles are *in* right now. So hey, let's throw down the musical penis-envy gauntlet and see whose is longest, once and for all.

5. Sufjan Stevens and Test Dept (Tie), 53 words

In fifth place, we have a tie between indie folk-rock auteur Sufjan Stevens and industrial pioneers Test Dept. (That's not an abbreviation, that's their actual name.) Both artists just happened to put out songs with titles that are fifty-three words long, so they're gonna have to share this one.

First, on Test Dept's 1987 album *A Good Night Out,* we have the second track, titled, "Long Live British Democracy Which Flourishes And Is Constantly Perfected Under The Immaculate Guidance Of The Great, Honourable, Generous And Correct Margaret Hilda Thatcher. She Is The Blue Sky In The Hearts Of All Nations. Our People Pay Homage And Bow In Deep Respect And Gratitude To Her. The Milk Of Human Kindness."

That's probably sarcasm, if you didn't gather and/or you're too young to know who Margaret Thatcher was.

Actual Song Length: 6:52

And on Sufjan Stevens's 2005 album, *Illinois* (sometimes called *Come On, Feel the Illinoise),* there's—again—the second track, which is called, "The Black Hawk War, or, How To Demolish an Entire Civilization and Still Feel Good About Yourself in the Morning, or, We Apologize for the Inconvenience but You're Going to Have to Leave Now, or, 'I Have Fought the Big Knives and Will Continue to Fight Them Until They Are Off Our Lands!'"

Goodness, two exceptionally long-titled songs and both are critical of government. The Black Hawk War, if you slept through American history, is not a reference to Black Hawk helicopters, but a war between the United States and a group of Native Americans led by a Sauk tribesman named Black Hawk. Google it sometime!

Actual Song Length: 2:15

4. irr. app. (ext.), 59 words

San Francisco-based indie experimental electronic artist Matt Waldron's main musical endeavor, irr. app. (ext.) (not an abbreviation either), self-released numerous CDs which made their way across the United States and netted him a fan base big enough to finally get wide releases for much of his work.

His third album, released in 1999, would have made it onto the Longest Album Titles list (at forty-three words) if we hadn't selfishly saved it for this one instead, and was named *Their Little Bones, Becoming Sharp, Find Repose But Fail To Avoid Worrying A Breach In The Ghostly Skin, The Which Separates That Above From That Below (This Being The Last And Final Seal) And Whereupon All Light Evacuated The Furnace. Several Consequences Ensue.* So hey, when you have a title like that, you'd better follow it up with something, right? The self-released album was originally limited to eighty copies, though Waldron recently sold another twenty, bringing the total up to 100. But hey, distribution methods aside, the guy has a hell of a thing for titles. Track six is called, "Concerning the Appearance of the Last World Mushroom: The Which Shall Promote and Inhabit the Time That Is the End of All Times, Even Subsequent to the Immersion of the World Beneath a Great Deluge of Waters, both Ginger'd and Sugary, and Across the Face of Which Its Manifestation Shall Engulf the Entirety of the Kingdom of the Earth."

So memorize that because there will be a test later. Remember, no second *e* in "ginger'd."

Actual Song Length: 13:50

3. Christine Lavin, 98 words

Folk music artist Christine Lavin may not be a household name, but she's one of the forepersons of the modern folk style. She's also the one who decided that playing folk music means you get to come up with obscenely long titles, apparently, because she was doing it all the way back in 1984. Track eight on her album *Future Fossils* is titled,

"Regretting What I Said to You When You Called Me At 11:00 on a Friday Morning to Tell Me That at 1:00 Friday Afternoon You're Gonna Leave Your Office, Go Downstairs, Hail a Cab to Go Out to the Airport to Catch a Plane to Go Skiing in the Alps for Two Weeks, Not that I Wanted to Go with You, I Wasn't Able to Leave Town, I'm Not a Very Good Skier, I Couldn't Expect You to Pay My Way, But After Going Out with You for Three Years, I Don't Like Surprises!! Subtitled: A Musical Apology."

They say if you're going to apologize, do it with a song title that's probably longer than the phone call it's referring to. "They" being us, just now. Also, it's probably in the Bible somewhere. (You're not going to check, are you? We thought not.)

Actual Song Length: 3:04

2. Speedranch and Jansky Noise, 126 words

Speedranch and Jansky Noise are two separate electronic artists who once decided to collaborate and make weird music. They don't have a band named Speedranch & Jansky Noise. That would just be ridiculous.

Their (to date) one and only combo album, *Mi^grate*, was released in 2003 and contains a song (thirteenth on the album) that they named, "Love, Exciting and New Come Aboard, We're Expecting You. Love, Life's Sweetest Reward. Let It Flow, It Floats Back to You. The Love Boat Will Soon Be Making Another Run, the Love Boat Promises Something for Everyone, Set a Course for Adventure, Your Mind on a New Romance. Love Won't Hurt Anymore, It's an Open Smile on a Friendly Shore. Yes Love! It's Love! The Love Boat Will Soon Be Making Another Run. The Love Boat Promises Something for Everyone, Set a Course for Adventure, Your Mind on a New Romance. Love Won't Hurt Anymore, It's an Open Smile on a Friendly Shore. It's Love! It's Love! It's Love! It's the Love Boat-Ah! It's the Love Boat-Ah! (Recorded Onboard the Love Boat With the Kitchen Staff)"

Look familiar? That's because it's the entire lyrics to the theme song of *The Love Boat.* So if you had that in mind as the title for your hit single someday, we're sorry to have to deliver the news this way.

Actual Song Length: 0:53. It takes longer to read the title.

1. ■ Brian Lavelle and Richard Youngs, 128 words

It seems that even "The Love Boat" can be outdone, however. Electronic musicians (they're all electronic musicians or folk singers, aren't they?) Brian Lavelle and Richard Youngs, another pair of occasional collaborators, released a series of albums titled *Radios.* The first volume, released in 1996, has a clever naming scheme where each track's title is a shorter variation on the one before it, with the track itself being shorter, as well. Of course, that has to start somewhere, and with the very first track we get:

"It and Distribution, Soldier Ant, Mention 'Active,' Nevertheless Would Update Strange Criterion-Fidelity; Does (Do?) Time/Sensitivity Direct Your 'One'—Analogous and Because Merely Sameness by Choosing Representation If Only Closeness, Respect, of Inevitable Abstraction Aspects about Radio—Certain Balance (Considerable?) Was Ranged Cortex (Ranged . . .) Neutrons and Even Complex Viruses Particularly the Idea-Ability Changes ('Invented') to Subtract Which Would Work Because Your Demands Monstrously, In Process—Calculator!—Concrete Construction Does Higher/Lower When Their God Computation Numbers and, God-like, the Recombination Has Become Months of Remark with Ugly Brain Because Multilevel (Lower) That Lower Molecular Field Physicist from the Press to You, Good, Given That Ground Level Brain Calculator Which Our Thin Processes Have Speeded a System (Doubt)—Description Level Forces of That Meagre Alphabet B."

By the end of it, they get down to a song just called "B.," which feels a lot less cumbersome, unless you have a really terrible lisp.

Actual Song Length: 23:32

The **Five** Longest English Palindromes

Palindromes are sentences, phrases, words, numbers, and whatever else that read the same backward as they do forward. For example, an old classic is, "A man, a plan, a canal, Panama," which reads "Hail, Lord Beelzebub, for he will usher forth an era of endless hedonism and debauchery" if you read it in reverse. Wait, no, we were reading it wrong. It's the same thing both ways. Totally.

Anyway, the thing about palindromes is that the longer they get, the less sense they're likely to make. "Madam, I'm Adam" is fine, but if you try to add a bunch of stuff to it, it's going to end up gibberish before long just due to the limited vocabulary and word placement options.

Naturally, that hasn't stopped these people, who decided to write ridiculously long palindromes for the hell of it. Don't expect to have fun reading them, though. Also, if you ever want to be a total jerk, write "a radar a," "mom dad mom," or "racecar" over and over for infinitely long palindromes and claim *they're* the longest in the world.

5. Will Helston: 5,000 words

Affectionately titled "A Gassy Obese Boy's Saga" (which sounds like the life story of that one cousin everyone has) and formerly just "Will's Palindrome," Will Helston's 5,000-word palindrome is far from the longest, but that's not for lack of trying. What's impressive is that it's one of the few palindromic stories that makes sense (kind of).

Helston claims to have worked on it off and on for a few years, starting from the middle (the word "sensuousness") and moving out from there. It begins with the sentences, "Star? Not I! Movie—it too has a star in or a cameo who wore mask—cast are livewires," and ends with, "As warts pop, a dosser I—we—vile rat, sack! Same row, oh woe! Macaroni, rats, as a hoot, tie. I vomit on rats." It's kind of funny, every story we try to write ends with people vomiting on rats, too. Isn't that hilarious? Or is that another one of those things we should keep to ourselves?

4. ■ David Stephens: "58,795 letters"

In 1980, writer David Stephens self-published a "novel" that consisted of a 58,795-letter-long (sometimes mistakenly reported as 58,795 *words*) palindrome, which he titled *Satire: Veritas*. Unfortunately, the book is long out of print (Stephens made each copy by hand, for $5 a pop, no less, which is about $15 today, so we wonder if he shouldn't have shopped around more or if we're just spoiled by Kinko's). As a result, extremely little is known about it other than its length and the fact that it existed.

If we assume an average length of five letters per word, we end up with approximately 11,759 words. As for the content, we're totally free to guess, but we're thinking it's probably a series of what looks like gibberish but is actually expertly chosen to be read both forward and backward, but still manages to tell the charming story of a macaque (those little monkeys with the adorable faces) who decides to become a little monkey fashion model, but ends up having to do terrible, unforgivable things (sex things, mostly) in order to secure his status in the modeling world. At least, that's what we'd write.

3. ■ Peter Norvig: 17,826 words

Peter Norvig, who is a director of research at Google, tried his hand at writing a long palindrome. Sort of, anyway. What he actually did was built a piece of software to do it for him, which is probably why he works at Google.

Based on a previous attempt made in 1984 by software developer Dan Hoey, who, using a computer, created a 540-word variation on the "A man, a plan, a canal, Panama" classic, Norvig's software used a much larger dictionary, which allowed it to make such a huge palindrome. What's more, his first attempt, in 2002, only reached 15,139 words. The 17,826-word version took another five years of refinement.

Seeing as it's built by a computer, it doesn't make any sense whatsoever, but hey, that's not what we're here for. Also based on the "A man, a plan" format, Norvig's palindrome begins, "A man, a plan, a cameo, Zena, bird, mocha," and ends with, "Lew, Orpah, Comdr, Ibanez, OEM, a canal, Panama." We totally did not see the "Panama" bit coming.

2. Gerald Berns: 31,358 words

But surely if a computer can manage a 17,000-word palindrome, given more time and a broader vocabulary, it could go even bigger, right? Well, probably, but a Mr. Gerald M. Burns was able to outdo Peter Norvig's computer-aided palindromes by creating a program with even stricter rules.

Unlike Norvig's palindrome software, which used a plain dictionary file and no particular rules, Berns's included rules like no repeated words or phrases, no single word could make up more than 1 percent of the whole, and no proper nouns or initials.

Despite all of the strict rules, his software was able to cook up a palindrome of 31,358 words that completely met all of his criteria. It's like deciding to play basketball one-handed, not out of necessity, but just to do it, and being way better at it than any two-handed player out there (which is the exact plot of our heartwarming basketball script, *Free Throw*).

The text begins with, "Eros abalone bad ace butt abandoned abate bag aside bah plain it rams again," (coincidentally, abandoned butts also figure heavily in *Free Throw*. Producers, call us) and ends with, "mania gas martini alpha bed i saga beta bade nod nab at tube cad a be no lab as ore." However, this palindrome isn't in the form of a sentence; it's just a list.

Fun fact: If you load this palindrome into a text to speech program, sync it up with *The Wizard of Oz*, and drop a few tabs of acid, your skin will turn into a different person who wants to cook Bananas Foster for you. We may have done this experiment incorrectly.

1. Lawrence Levine: 31,594 words

Just barely squeaking out a win over Bern's palindrome is Lawrence Levine's 1980 palindromic novel, *Dr. Awkward & Olson in Oslo*. And yes, it is an actual novel, with characters and everything. Dr. Awkward (the titular villain), Olson in Oslo (his nemesis), and private detective Sam X. Xmas (plus his girlfriend Mabel E. Bam) try to outdo each other, all while using odd turns of phrase and archaic language while speaking. (Convenient for palindromes, not so convenient for casual readers, as it happens.)

Naturally, it doesn't make the greatest amount of sense ever, but hey, it was constructed by hand, so eat that, computers. You can't stick wires in our brains and jam us in weird, amniotic vats just yet, although that does sound oddly comfortable and we'd probably be up for at least discussing it over some lunch.

Dr. Awkward's villainous scheme (whatever it is) is thwarted by Xmas and Olson, and he is tried and brought to justice. So, y'know, hooray and stuff. But we'll tell you a little secret: If you just immediately start rereading every sentence backward from the beginning, you can spoil the ending for yourself pretty quickly and save some time.

The Longest Palindromic Poem

Not every palindrome is total gibberish, but they do end up sounding like some strange, experimental poetry. Taking advantage of that fact, several writers have made palindromic poetry a thing, and the longest one to date was written by comedian and regular Comedy Central fixture Demetri Martin.

His poem, "Dammit, I'm Mad," is a 224-word palindrome about (naturally) a dissatisfied narrator who is questioning the nature of good and evil and where he falls in the continuum. It's actually not a comedic poem (despite mentioning urine *twice*) and is a little on the oddly creepy side. We can't reprint it here, but a quick Google should turn it up. It kind of sounds like something that would be read aloud in a spooky old church by a guy in a pig mask.

The **Five**
Longest Sentences Ever Published

Have you ever talked to an old person who just rambles from subject to subject without pause? One minute it's about how their kids don't appreciate them, and the next they're talking about how they used work with elephants in the circus and fell in love with Reese Witherspoon or something.

The literary version of that, of course, is the long sentence. It's fallen out of favor in recent years due to a focus on short descriptions and clipped dialogue, but it used to be a kind of challenge, especially for the stream-of-consciousness Modernist writers (those people your high school English teacher wanted you to read, but you just pretended to, and you still got an *A* because the teacher didn't understand what the hell they were about, either).

Here, we have the five longest sentences ever published. Naturally, there are blogs and YouTube comments and such that run far longer without a speck of punctuation, but we'll forget about those, because that way madness lies.

5. *Absalom, Absalom!*, 1,288 words

William Faulkner's 1936 Southern Gothic novel (and some say his greatest work, but *The Sound and the Fury* will totally fight you for saying that) *Absalom, Absalom!* is not only an allegorical look at Southern culture pre- and post-Civil War (some of us paid attention in Southern Lit) as viewed through the lens of the Sutpen family, but it also happens to contain one of the longest sentences published in English, and that totally ties in to the narrative in that slavery went on way too long, much like the sentence, and . . . we're just totally trying to BS our way through this now. (Sorry for getting your hopes up, former professors.)

The sentence, which can be found in Chapter 6 (not Chapter 8 as is sometimes claimed) begins with, "Just exactly like father if father had known as much about it the night before I went out there as he did . . . " and ends with " . . . the old fine figure of the man who once galloped on the black thoroughbred about that domain two boundaries of which the eye could not see from any point."

You're probably exhausted just from reading those short excerpts, but you get the idea. Probably. Maybe. Right? Look, it wouldn't make a whole lot more sense if you read the whole thing, so let's just all take the time we saved to go for a lovely nature walk, cool? (We'll stay inside while you guys go, because outside is all sunny and stuff.)

4. *Ulysses*, 12,931 words

Ulysses, or as it's commonly known by English majors, "Seinfeld: The Book Where Nothing Happens," or "*The Odyssey* if it were about a dopey Irish guy instead of a badass Greek," is James Joyce's 1922 novel that tells the story of Leopold Bloom (mostly) as he wanders around Dublin for a day and kind of acts like a huge wiener.

The final vignette of the book (commonly referred to as "Penelope" these days) features the sleepless thoughts of Leopold's wife, Molly Bloom, who . . . well, she's got some issues (several of which are kind of Leopold's fault, but we digress). In the traditional Modernist style, Molly's thoughts are transcribed directly as they occur, as if the invisible voice inside your head (everyone has one of those, right?) had a megaphone pointed directly at a creepy Irish writer. (And he was creepy. Have you ever read his letters to Nora Barnacle? That stuff is disgusting. Take it down a notch, fella. Er, take it down retroactively, because you've been dead a long time now.)

Molly's soliloquy, as it's called, features a mere two uninterrupted sentences (as defined by the use of periods), the longer of which is 12,931 words long. The shorter would still beat Faulkner, since it was 11,282 words long. (Some scholars argue that the soliloquy is actually eight sentences and only two of them actually have end punctuation, but *Ulysses* would still be in fourth place on our list because the longest is still 4,391 words.)

Now imagine how much more famous James Joyce would be if he just used all of his time writing extremely long, filthy letters to random people (famous in jail, we mean).

3. *The Rotters' Club*, 13,955 words

The only contemporary novel on this list, Jonathan Coe's 2001 novel *The Rotters' Club* is a semi-autobiographical take on three British teenagers' experiences growing up in the 1970s. In America, that meant disco music and *Star Wars*. In England, that meant the punk subculture and labor strikes. We don't mean to overstate the terribleness of disco, but it kind of sounds like both countries got the short end in some way.

Still, *The Rotters' Club* contains a 13,955 word sentence, which is just over 1,000 words longer than Joyce's longest sentence. According to Coe, he was inspired by another work with an even longer sentence (stay tuned for that one) but had no idea he'd be outdoing James Joyce (who probably wrote him a disturbing letter from beyond the grave) and creating the world's longest literary sentence in English in the process.

When read aloud on BBC Radio, the sentence took one hour and seventeen minutes to finish, which means you could just barely fit the whole thing on a single audio CD (those cap out at one hour and twenty minutes), which must have required some expert timing on the audiobook version. Otherwise, how would they find a stopping point for the disc switch? (We assume the reader is probably just dead from being unable to take a breath, anyway.)

2. *Dancing Lessons for the Advanced in Age*, 22,347 words

The aforementioned work that Jonathan Coe cited as the inspiration behind the long sentence in *The Rotters' Club, Dancing Lessons for the Advanced in Age* (or *Taneční hodiny pro starší a pokročilé*) is a 1964 novel (despite the self-help-sounding title) by Czech writer Bohumil Hrabal. The entire book is a single, uninterrupted sentence made up of all 22,347 words. (Since the book is in Czech, it doesn't qualify for the longest *English* sentence, but we're just going for longest published sentences, so eat it. Also, the length may vary depending on what language you use. Obviously, we used the English translation.)

The novel is simply the unnamed narrator telling of his life and loves, military service, and so on, to a group of sunbathing women. Therefore, we can deduce that the narrator is probably a total creepshow who breathlessly recounted his life story to women who were unable to get away from him, and we are simply left to read it. Fun for the whole family.

At 128 pages, the book could theoretically be read in one session, which is likely preferable, because otherwise you're going to get super pissed while looking for a stopping point. Even then, you're probably going to have to backtrack to figure out where the hell you are, like the weirdo old man has been talking the whole time and you're just now coming back into the conversation. Congratulations, you're reading "Conversations with Old Relatives You Don't Remember Ever Meeting Before: The Novel."

1. *The Gates of Paradise*, 40,000 words

Finally, at nearly double the length of *Dancing Lessons for the Advanced in Age*, we have *The Gates of Paradise,* a 1960 Polish novel by Jerzy

Andrzejewski, which is probably the most Polish name ever, and anyone else trying for that title should just go home and sulk.

The Gates of Paradise (*Bramy raju* in the original Polish) is a 40,000-word novel made up of two sentences. Before you get all excited, though, one of the sentences is only four words long (five words when translated into English): "And they marched all night." The other, naturally, is one nigh-endless sentence that tells the tale of a group of children who have been recruited into the thirteenth-century Children's Crusade.

If you don't remember your history, the Children's Crusade was the (possibly completely fictitious) "crusade" where large bands of children supposedly decided to try to "convert" Muslims in the Holy Lands to Christianity (note that in previous Crusades, "convert" actually meant "wantonly kill"). No one will ever know if the kids would have been successful (or if they would have actually murdered people over religion just like grownups did), because they purportedly got picked up along the way by slave boats and sold into captivity. Insert sad trombone noise here.

Again, modern historians hold that the whole thing probably never happened or was greatly exaggerated, but that wasn't important to Andrzejewski, because he wasn't trying to pull off a historical novel, but instead intended to draw parallels between the Children's Crusade and the corruption and hopelessness in Communist Poland at the time. It takes a special kind of author to take a story about kids being kidnapped and killed or enslaved and somehow make it *even more depressing.*

The Five Longest Brand Names in the English Language

There are a lot of important decisions that go into a good brand name. Apple's quite good at it, with short but sweet product names like iPad and Mac OS X. Microsoft, on the other hand, tends to be terrible at it, with behemoth titles like Visual Basic Studio and Internet Explorer (though they've gotten better at it in recent years, with simpler product names like Surface and Xbox 360).

What gets worse is when the companies insert their own name into the brand name or add a bunch of useless adjectives. Can you imagine how unpopular the McRib would be if we had to call it The Delicious McDonald's Rib Sandwich with Unspecific Meat Sauce? Short names sell (as do artificial limitations, but we'll leave that alone). Long names rarely work. Except, well, *sometimes* they do, and they end up just being an everyday thing with an unwieldy name, like the following.

5. Tie: *Oxford English Dictionary* and *Encyclopaedia Britannica*, 23 letters

It's a tie in fifth place for two of the juggernauts of English language reference titles. *Oxford English Dictionary* and *Encyclopaedia Britannica* both have twenty-three letters in their name (unless you put that æ symbol in Encyclopædia, which would bring it down to twenty-two, but we're not feeling very generous today).

Oxford does force their company name into the *Oxford English Dictionary* brand name, but otherwise it'd just be *English Dictionary*, which isn't very explanatory for a book that's literally just explanations of things.

Encyclopaedia Britannica, meanwhile, has named their product directly after the company (actually, it's the other way around, but whatever), so they're kind of stuck with it. Even the literal English alternative, *British*

Encyclopedia, is pretty rough at nineteen letters. Maybe we should have developed a more streamlined name for encyclopedias at some point in the history of our language.

4. ▪ I Can't Believe It's Not Butter!, 24 letters

Technically, I Can't Believe It's Not Butter! could be tied with the number three slot, but since they both have a tendency to use varying amounts of punctuation in their names, we had to draw a line somewhere and split them into two entries. Also, they don't go together as well as English reference books, as you'll see.

I Can't Believe It's Not Butter! is one of the more memorable faux butter products available at your local supermarket today (please ignore the check from Unilever stuffed in our pockets, that's for a lawsuit settlement regarding some extreme, ahem, "gastrointestinal distress" caused by consuming some of their nonfood products when said products were not clearly labeled as Do Not Eat) due to its commercials featuring Fabio and the annoying-voiced neighbor from *Will & Grace* (Ron Swanson's evil ex-wife, Tammy, on *Parks and Recreation*, for you kids too young to remember *Will & Grace*).

Although having a conversational-sounding name for your product might seem like a good idea, in practice it's kind of a pain in the ass, because we can guarantee that no one in history has said, "Hey, hon, could you hand me the I Can't Believe It's Not Butter! out of the fridge?" They're far more likely to just say, "Get the butter, it's pizza night," whether it's *actually* butter or not.

Also, if you've ever wondered what I Can't Believe (blah blah, we're tired of typing that) is if it's not butter, the answer is lots and lots of vegetable oil.

3. ▪ Gee, Your Hair Smells Terrific, 25 letters

The other conversationally named product of the latter half of the twentieth century, Gee, Your Hair Smells Terrific is the only failed product on this list, as it turns out. Popular in the 1970s, this one died with disco and is now only found in the Philippines and retro curiosity shops.

You're probably not familiar with this one if you're under the age of fifty or so, so we'll give a little background. Gee, Your Hair Smells Terrific was a scented shampoo and conditioner marketed toward teenage girls in the '70s. It came in rounded pink bottles that vaguely resemble today's Pepto-Bismol bottles, which is probably how we ended up passing one around the office and drinking out of it last Christmas.

It, too, was famous for its commercials and print ads, but in this case for all the wrong reasons. They featured awkward teens who were apparently compelled to sniff the hair of random girls, like how dogs sniff each others' butts or something. Nowadays, the product would have to be renamed, "Gee, your hair smells like you're terrified because I'm super close to you and sniffing deeply and now you need to get in my windowless van."

2. ▪ Sony Entertainment Television, 27 letters

This one may be a bit of a mystery to our American readers. In various countries and regions around the world (England, India, East Asia, Latin America, etc.) Sony operates their own television network (usually on cable/satellite), much like Paramount and Warner Bros. used to do before they combined it into the monstrous offspring that is The CW.

Although the exact programming varies by region (in the UK, it's strangely marketed toward 20-something women, for example), the channel focuses on TV shows and movies produced and distributed by Sony. Go figure.

But instead of just calling it Sony TV (which we guess might be confused with their actual TV manufacturing business), The Sony Channel (which might get confused with the more widely available Sony Movie Channel), or some completely different name (but then you wouldn't know it's from Sony, duh), they went with mouthful of Sony Entertainment Television, because what the hell, right?

At least they're wise enough to abbreviate it as SET in most of the advertising materials, but that does draw unfortunate connotations to the Egyptian god Set, who murdered his brother and stole his throne. (Please note that we're probably the only people who have ever even mentioned that, much less cared to make the connection.)

1. ■ Morgan Stanley Wealth Management, 29 letters

In the aftermath of the 2008 financial crisis, Wall Street underwent a big game of Three-card Monte/musical chairs where everyone merged and got bought out and transfigured, *Akira*-style, into all new financial behemoths. One of those was Morgan Stanley, who purchased a controlling share in Citigroup's Wealth Management unit ("wealth management" being a cutesy way of saying "piggy bank for rich people") called Smith Barney, which is so similar to the name of Neil Patrick Harris's character on *How I Met Your Mother* that now we can't stop picturing him in charge of this company.

Afterward, Morgan Stanley christened the new division Morgan Stanley Smith Barney, which almost makes Sterling Cooper Draper Pryce sound downright reasonable (almost). The name was widely mocked for being obscenely long and for telling customers nothing at all about the services they offered, and so Morgan Stanley listened to half of that criticism and re-named the brand Morgan Stanley Wealth Management in late 2012, bumping the name from twenty-four letters (which would have tied it with I Can't Believe it's Not Butter!) to twenty-nine letters, which rockets it straight to first place. Well done, everybody.

The Longest Law Firm Name in the World

Having a good, memorable name for your law firm makes writing cheesy TV jingles super easy. Since many of them are named after the partners involved, however, that can make things a little difficult, especially if they have an embarrassing last name like Boner. (But seriously, we'd have Boner & Boner rise to the bench for us any time, if you know what we mean.)

What gets even more ridiculous is when you have a *lot* of partners, like the famous L.A. entertainment law firm Ziffren, Brittenham, Branca, Fischer, Gilbert-Lurie, Stiffelman, Cook, Johnson, Lande & Wolf, which not only has the longest law firm name in the United States, but also counts major names in the music and movie industries as its clients. Out of only twenty-three employees, nearly half are partners, giving the firm a name seventy-two letters long. They must be really chummy with whoever does their stationery.

The Eight Longest Made-Up Words in Fiction

In contrast to the longest words in the dictionary, these are terms made up for a singular purpose and pretty much never intended to be used by anyone ever again, except us, right now, for you, because we think you're kind of cute and want to know if you want to go out sometime. (You don't have to answer right now. Just think about it.)

These words, more commonly referred to as "coinages," usually aren't in the dictionary unless they happen to get used enough to make it into the common lexicon (one of these has, but we'll get to that). There's an excellent chance you'll never hear these again, so you should savor this moment. Turn on some nice music, have a glass of your favorite beverage (we're going with Hawaiian Punch in a wine glass), and take it easy while we massage your brain with gibberish words.

8. Aldiborontiphoscophornio, 24 letters

WHAT IT MEANS: It's actually the name of a courtier who becomes a prostitute for the Queen (along with fellow courtier Rigdum Funnidos) in the play *Chrononhotonthologos* by eighteenth-century English poet Henry Carey. The play, a parody of the Greek-style tragedies that were popular at the time, concerns King Chrononhotonthologos and his wife, Queen Fadladinida. (Yes, all of the characters have ridiculous names.)

The play was meant to be a political satire as well, but we can't get into all that here. Suffice to say, it was hilarious and biting in its time, and now it's still pretty hilarious, actually.

7. Metaphysico-theologo-cosmonigology, 32 letters

WHAT IT MEANS: It's a fictional school of philosophy invented by French writer Voltaire in *Candide*. Candide, the title character, has a mentor, Dr.

Pangloss, who is a firm advocate of the school of thought, which is actually a thinly veiled attack on a real philosophy known as "optimism," which is not to be confused with being constantly cheery.

Optimism is the belief that this world—our world—is the best of all possible worlds (or the optimum), because although terrible things do happen in it, it is usually the fault of humans, and when it isn't, it's for a greater outcome in the end. Voltaire rejected the idea as being oversimplified and, well, kind of silly. Dr. Pangloss, thus, is a dope whose beliefs Candide spends the novel attempting to distance himself from.

6. Supercalifragilisticexpialidocious, 34 letters

WHAT IT MEANS: Come on, you know this one, and it's actually in the dictionary. It means "we wanted to mess with Dick Van Dyke so we made up a really long word he'd have to say in his ridiculous fake accent." Sure, the film says it means "something to say when you have nothing to say," but we usually just throw out random swears when that happens.

Technically, if you break the word down into its parts, it does sort of have a meaning, which is frequently given as "atoning for educability through delicate beauty," which basically means it doesn't matter if you're smart if you're nice to look at, and while that's not entirely untrue, it doesn't fit in with the vibe of the song, so that's probably not meant to be taken too seriously.

5. Praetertranssubstantiationalistically, 37 letters

WHAT IT MEANS: A fake religious term created by writer Mark McShane for his 1963 novel, *Untimely Ripped,* which we're assuming is not a memoir about male modeling. Transubstantiation *is* a real thing in the Catholic Church. It's the belief that the bread and wine consumed during Holy

Communion are actually magically transformed into the flesh and blood of Christ, which seems gross, we'll admit, but that's just how Catholics roll.

Praetertranssubtantiation, however, is McShane's term for "surpassing" transubstantiation. The book's long out of print, so we have no idea exactly what that means (according to Guinness World Records, it is in there, though, for what it's worth), so we're just going to assume it's when you get to the point where you say, "No thanks, man. I'm good on flesh and blood. Me and Jesus have an understanding. We're cool."

4. Osseocarnisanguineoviscericartilagi- nonervomedullary, 51 letters

WHAT IT MEANS: Created by English writer Thomas Love Peacock for his 1815 novel *Headlong Hall*, osseocarnisanguineoviscericartilaginonervomedullary is, essentially, a really long word for describing something as having the characteristics of a human body.

The word breaks down into the classical Latin terms used for various systems of the body, so all Peacock really did was string them all together into a ridiculous word. And he did it two other times with the Greek terms when he coined osteosarchaematosplanchnochondroneuromuelous (forty-four letters) and tethippharmatelesipedioploctipophillary (thirty-nine letters) as well. Hell, and we barely got off our couches and came into the office today.

3. Aequeosalinocalcalinoceraceoalumi- nosocupreovitriolic, 52 letters

WHAT IT MEANS: A word purportedly used to describe the waters at the spas in Bath, England, coined by eighteenth-century medical writer Dr. Edward Strother. When? No one seems to know. In what context? No idea. Apparently, after decades of copy-pasting the same sparse info over and over (we found books and magazines from the 1970s that literally had the exact same info we have today), it seems that more details on the origins of the word are lost.

The Oxford Dictionaries website once had a brief bit about it (no further info than what we've given, though) but has since inexplicably removed it from their site. Guinness World Records has claimed it's real, but we have no way of verifying it. We're telling you this because if it turns out to be crap later, we can say we smelled BS. But, hey, it is a word, and someone made it up at some point, so let's move on.

The word can be broken down into its Latin roots. *Aequeo* means equal (not water, as claimed by some), *salino* means salty, *calcalino* is calcified, *ceraceno* means waxy, *aluminoso* is aluminum-like, *cupreo* means coppery, and *vitriolic* is an old-fashioned word for sulfuric. And . . . actually, that water sounds freaking terrible. Calcium and sulphur? Coppery taste? (Hopefully it's not the color that's coppery.) We're thinking this word wasn't actually meant to compliment the spas at Bath, but Dr. Strother (if he was, indeed, the creator) was just too nice to call it "piss-smelling garbage water."

2. Ullhodturdenweirmudgaardgringnirurdrmol-nirfenrirlukkilokkibaugimandodrrerinsurtkrin-mgernrackinarockar, 101 letters

Ooh, our editors hate this one. This word was invented by our favorite weird Irishman, James Joyce, in his impenetrable novel *Finnegans Wake*. This word, the final of ten so-called "thunder words," is meant to be an onomatopoeic representation of the fall of the Norse Gods (and is, in fact, just made up of several of their names). Come on, that was totally obvious, wasn't it? You didn't need us to tell you that.

The other nine thunder words, which we will list below to make our layout people sweat a little (and possibly break your e-book reader), are each meant to resemble various historical, religious, and philosophical concepts that Joyce was trying to convey in individual, giant words. (All the thunder words are 100 letters long except for the one at the beginning of this entry, which is 101 letters.)

* Bababadalgharaghtakamminarronnkonnbronntonnerronntuonnthunntrovarrhounawnskawntoohoohoordenenthurnuk
* Perkodhuskurunbarggruauyagokgorlayorgromgremmitghundhurthrumathunaradidillifaititillibumullunukkunun
* Klikkaklakkaklaskaklopatzklatschabattacreppycrottygraddaghsemmihsammihnouithappluddyappladdypkonpkot
* Bladyughfoulmoecklenburgwhurawhorascortastrumpapornanennykocksapastippatappatupperstrippuckputtanach
* Thingcrooklyexineverypasturesixdixlikencehimaroundhersthemaggerbykinkinkankanwithdownmindlookingated
* Lukkedoerendunandurraskewdylooshoofermoyportertooryzooysphalnabortansporthaokansakroidverjkapakkapuk
* Bothallchoractorschumminaroundgansumuminarumdrumstrumtruminahumptadumpwaultopoofoolooderamaunsturnup
* Pappappapparrassannuaragheallachnatullaghmonganmacmacmacwhackfalltherdebblenonthedubblandaddydoodled
* Husstenhasstencaffincoffintussemtossemdamandamnacosaghcusaghhobixhatouxpeswchbechoscashlcarcarcaract

If you're feeling compelled to "decode" any of these, get in line. Literary scholars and linguists have been attempting to do just that for nearly a century, and several of the thunder words still aren't completely understood. We'd wager Joyce just fell asleep on the typewriter for some of these, but his vision troubles reportedly led to him writing his later works on butcher paper in huge print with a red crayon or charcoal pencil, and now our hands are cramping just thinking of that.

1. Lopadotemachoselachogaleokranioleipsanodrimhypotrimmatosilphioparaomelitokatakechymenokichlepikossyphophattoperisteralektryonoptekephalliokigklopeleiolagoiosiraiobaphetraganopterygon, 182 letters

This is not only the longest word on this list, but also happens to be the oldest. From the Greek comic play Ἐκκλησιάζουσαι (*The Ecclesiazusae*, or *Assemblywomen* in English), written in 391 B.C., comes this 182-letter word that describes, of all things, a fictional Greek food.

Greek playwright and poet Aristophanes was one of the most famous writers of comedy of his time, and we guess you'd have to have quite the sense of humor to come up with a word like "λοπαδοτεμαχοσελαχογαλ εοκρανιολειψανοδριμυποτριμματοσιλφιοκαραβομελιτοκατακεχυμενο κιχλεπικοσσυφοφαττοπεριστεραλεκτρυονοπτοκεφαλλιοκιγκλοπελειο λαγῳοσιραιοβαφητραγανοπτερύγων" (the original Greek version of the above).

What's more, it really doesn't have anything to do with the plot of the play, which involves Athenian women fooling the Assembly (the major lawmaking body of Athens) into allowing them to rule the city. After they manage that, they begin a socialist platform that takes care of all Athenians and institute a free love policy that requires that all men sleep with an ugly woman before a beautiful one. Minus that last part, it's basically hippie central.

The mega-word comes at the very end of the play, where the audience is invited to take part in a feast thrown by the women, and the dish is called out by name for no particular reason. It's kind of like Aristophanes just decided to screw with the actors at the very end for kicks.

Oh, and there are recipes available if you're interested, but we'll warn you that it includes fun ingredients like rotten sharks' heads and roasted pigeon. Yum!

The Six Best-Selling Novels of All Time

You know that one book that *everyone* has read except you? Last year it was the *Fifty Shades* series. Next year, who knows, but if we're escalating in our societal fetishes, we can only assume it will involve bestiality, so we're going ahead and writing our entry into that field right now. We're calling it *The Jockey's Jockeys*. It's sure to be a bestseller.

Anyway, as it happens, there are actually some books that almost everyone really *has* read. Er, that we know of, at least. Tracking book sales is a pretty modern thing, so it's not an exact science or anything. Still, these are the novels that have seen the most eyeballs since we've been keeping up with that kind of thing.

6. Agatha Christie, *And Then There Were None* (100 million copies sold)

And Then There Were None, also known as "the most offensive title on your grandma's bookshelf" (seriously, the original title was *Ten Little* <insert extremely offensive term for black people here>, because apparently we took our racism *very* seriously back then), is, by far, Agatha Christie's best-known novel.

Published in 1939 (long after you'd think the *n*-word would be a bad word in England, but what do we know), the novel tells the story of ten people on a secluded island who are killed one by one. Yes, just like the *Family Guy* episode with James Woods (like all of them don't have James Woods these days).

Not only is the book Christie's most popular, but it's actually the most popular mystery novel ever written (and it's a for-real mystery, none of that faux-thriller "mystery" stuff). Sorry, Sherlock Holmes. Maybe if Arthur Conan Doyle hadn't been stuck on doing short stories instead. (And maybe if he'd thrown more racism around. Okay, we'll quit harping on that now.)

5. Cao Xueqin, *Dream of the Red Chamber* (100 million copies sold)

This one's technically a tie with *And Then There Were None,* but since we can't write about both simultaneously (we tried), we just picked one to be in front of the other. Congratulations, China!

Cao Xueqin's *Dream of the Red Chamber* is a bit of a distant relative of *Romance of the Three Kingdoms,* which we mentioned back in the Longest Novels list. Both, along with *Water Margin* and *Journey to the West,* are frequently called the "Four Great Classical Novels" in Chinese literature. Each contains detailed depictions of life in the era in which they were written. *Dream of the Red Chamber* is the last of the four, published in 1791 (though handwritten copies floated around before then) and thus reflects Chinese life during the Qing Dynasty, the last Imperial Dynasty of China.

The novel tells of two wealthy, aristocratic families and their rise and eventual fall in favor with the emperor. Meanwhile, the thirty-odd individual members of the families have their own successes and failures (mostly failures, since their families are kind of falling apart). Essentially, it's your typical family drama, like *Dallas* or something, only it's set over 200 years ago and in China.

The novel is wildly popular in China, even spurring its own scholarly field known as "Redology," researchers of which have published hundreds of critical dissections and biographies of Cao Xueqin. So he's beloved by scholars and other nerds, like Hemingway, but sells like Harry Potter. We'd say, "Just wait until we have one of those kinds of authors here," but . . .

4. J. R. R. Tolkien, *The Hobbit* (over 100 million copies sold)

We have already had one. Again, this would technically be a tie with the previous two, but since Peter Jackson has made the story popular once again with his film versions, we assume this one's selling like gangbusters these days and has probably surpassed the 100 million figure, which is about five years old.

One of the most popular and influential (especially to metal bands and other geek types) fantasy novels ever written, *The Hobbit* tells of Bilbo Baggins (Frodo's cousin in the books, uncle in the movies), Gandalf, and a whole freaking ton of dwarves (whose names you'll never remember) and their quest to kill a gold-loving dragon. (Seriously, man, what do dragons even need money for? You are a *freaking dragon*. Gold and jewels mean *nothing* to you.)

It's pretty straightforward, as far as fantasy books go, but in 1937, no one else was really taking the genre seriously and, let's face it, it's a good story with good characters, and you can never undervalue that. Anyway, from Leonard Nimoy's screwy "Ballad of Bilbo Baggins" song on up to the Rankin/Bass animated film version and today's big, fancy, special effects–and Martin Freeman–laden trilogy, the book has kind of been a huge deal. And man, did you hear about the sequel Tolkien wrote?

3. Antoine de Saint-Exupéry, *The Little Prince* (140 million copies sold)

The Little Prince (or *Le Petit Prince*) is a 1943 novella (which isn't technically a novel, we know, hush) by French writer and aristocrat Antoine de Saint-Exupéry, although you wouldn't know he was an aristocrat (actually a count) if you met him. He was not only a badass pilot, but when the French Air Force was shut down due to France's surrender to Germany during World War II, he actually came to America to try to persuade them to join in and beat up some Nazis. In the end, it was Pearl Harbor and not Saint-Exupéry (who was presumed dead when his plane was lost flying a mission in 1944) who got them there, but we like to think that, in some small way, he's the reason we have *Inglourious Basterds* now.

But, being an all-around awesome-sounding guy aside, he was also a hugely popular and talented writer, and he kept cranking out works all through the war. *The Little Prince,* published a year before his death, was obviously the most popular by far. It's technically a children's book (and was also illustrated by Saint-Exupéry himself), but in the same way that *Where The Wild Things Are* is a children's book, by which we mean that it's still worth reading as an adult.

The book tells a cutesy story of a pilot who crashes in the Sahara Desert and meets a prince, who comes from a tiny asteroid-planet. The prince tells the pilot how he came to Earth (he was bored) and explains all the various things he's learned since his arrival. It sounds simple, but it's actually got a lot of depth and nuance to it. Also, it's totally available in, like, every language ever. (Maybe not Klingon. Sorry, nerds.) Go read it to the favorite kid(s) in your life, or your dog, or someone you're into. Or just yourself, we guess. (It's okay, we read it to the office aquarium.)

2. J. R. R. Tolkien, *The Lord of the Rings* (150 million copies sold)

"Wait a second," you cry. "Isn't *The Lord of the Rings* a trilogy?" Good question, and actually, no. As it happens, the novel was always intended to be in a single volume by Tolkien and his publishers. Unfortunately, post-wartime paper shortages led to it being split into three volumes (in some regions of the world, it was as many as seven).

For the record, most sales numbers only count sales of the one-volume or three-in-one editions and not copies of the individual volumes, so we're actually only seeing sales of the entire novel. Who knows how many more there'd be if they counted everyone who dropped one of them in the bath and had to replace just that book. (We actually dropped all three books in the office toilet at various points, so we're down for two sets ourselves.)

You probably know the story if you're one of the $3 billion worth of people who saw the films. Frodo, cousin/nephew of Bilbo from *The Hobbit*, takes the ring his cousin/uncle found in the possession of a super-dirty little creature called Gollum sixty years earlier, and tries to toss it into a volcano. Along the way, there's wizards, elves, dwarves, orcs, and all that kind of stuff that made prog rock fans in the '70s and '80s need clean pants.

Published nearly twenty years after *The Hobbit,* the novel has easily outstripped the original's popularity. Who says sequels are always bad? (Anyone who's seen *The Godfather, Part III,* we're guessing.)

1. Charles Dickens, *A Tale of Two Cities* ■ (200 million copies sold)

Weren't expecting that, were you? We bet you're wondering where *Harry Potter* is, and the answer is that, while the series as a whole has sold marvelously at 450 million copies, no individual Harry Potter book appears to have sold over 100 million. (The average for all seven books is just shy of sixty-five million each, and the publishers don't put out stats for the individual books.)

Anyway, we're here to talk about a different British writer right now, and that's Charles Dickens. Although *A Christmas Carol, Oliver Twist,* and *Great Expectations* get more cultural recognition, Dickens's 1859 novel *A Tale of Two Cities* is his bestseller. Weird, right? The bleak, non-comedic historical fiction that concludes (spoiler alert!) with one of the main characters getting guillotined ends up being way more popular than anything else.

Part of the reason is that, while the book is quite popular in English, it's also extremely popular in French, seeing as the novel is set against the backdrop of the French revolution. In fact, it's very popular all over Europe and the rest of the world, whereas many of Dickens's other works are mostly only popular in English-speaking countries.

So if you want to write a bestselling book, it seems the answer is to tell a character drama set against the backdrop of a major war, real or fictional, doesn't matter. Oh, hey, isn't that also the story to every top-grossing, critically acclaimed movie ever, from *Gone with the Wind* to *Avatar*? We thought so. Just remember to thank us for all of your awards.

The **Five**
Oldest Curse Words
We Still Use

There's nothing like a good old swear word to break the monotony between songs at your kid's Christmas pageant, but did you know that some of those words that make your mama blush are actually pretty old? They weren't just fooling around on *Deadwood*. They really did use those words. In fact, some curses could have popped up in shows set in earlier times and still have been historically accurate.

Now, due to a certain civil suit (and possible violation of some U.N. propaganda laws), we're not allowed to actually print some of these words, but you'll know what we're talking about. Hopefully. You #$%@.

5. Sh*t

Before you open your mouth, it's always a good idea to know your you-know-what. So we're going to tell you all about it. But not, like, in a breaking into your bathroom kind of way. We learned our lesson about that two Christmases ago.

Anyway, the *s*-word has quite the history behind it. People have been referring to their dookies with similar words for centuries. First, let's talk about excrement. (Boy, *that's* a sentence we didn't think we'd hear again so soon after our court-mandated therapy sessions concluded.) Specifically, the Latin word *excernere*, which means "to separate," as in to separate your waste from your body. It was a common enough term in Ancient Rome for taking the Browns to the Super Bowl, if you follow our meaning.

But Old English had a similar term, and with a similar definition. *Scite* (pronounced similarly to how Scottish people pronounce the *s*-word today, like "kite") also meant "to separate" or "to cut," the latter of which brings some unpleasant imagery to mind. But here's the thing: despite the Roman conquests of Europe, we didn't get it from them. In fact, Proto-Germanic, which predates Roman incursions into Europe, had the word *skit*, which had the same meaning as *scite*. So how did both cultures end up using similar terms for their poo?

It turns out that the mother tongue of both languages, Proto-Indo-European, has the answer. As far back as 3000 B.C., the word *skheid*, which also meant "to separate," was used as a term for making brownies. That's over 5,000 years of sh*t, friends and neighbors. Think about that next time you're in the bathroom for a while.

4. Ass

Hey, all right, we looked over the court documents and we're still allowed to say ass! Let's celebrate that ass! Much like the *s*-word, ass is far older than you'd believe. Of course, they say ass in the Bible, but they're talking about donkeys, so that doesn't count, as our Sunday School teachers had to constantly point out. That form of ass actually has a totally different etymology from the butt form of ass that's frequently shouted at televised football games.

Donkey-ass (keep your mind on the subject at hand, please) is most likely from the Sumerian word *ansu* and just happened to merge with the other ass over the centuries. The other ass, as you might know if you've ever watched British TV and movies, was originally "arse" and the American accent has rounded it down over time so much that even Britain is saying "ass" now, too.

Arse comes from the Proto-Germanic word *arsaz*, which also migrated into Old Norse and High German (*ars*), Old Frisian (*ers*), and even Ancient Greek (*orros* or ὅρρος). That's some impressive ass movement, and it hasn't even really changed, definition or pronunciation. You could probably call some old logger in ancient Europe an ass and he wouldn't even have to pause before pounding the crap out of you and skinning you with his teeth or something.

But, of course, that's not quite the beginning of ass, either, because it seems our good friend Proto-Indo-European, the root language for most of the Western world, also had some ass going on in the form of "*h₃érsos.*" PIE, which is a delicious abbreviation, didn't have a written language that we know of, so that's just a pronunciation key for what scholars think it probably sounded like, but it sounds something like arse. Sort of. We think.

3. Piss

Two words in a row that we aren't legally prohibited from repeating in written form! Piss is like the *s*-word's slightly less gross (in that you can do it in front of your friends as long as your back is turned [sorry, ladies], and if you're out in the middle of the woods or in the yard and drunk at a party) but still pretty gross cousin, and it also happens to be pretty old, as well.

You may recall, if you read it at any point in school, that in Chaucer's *The Canterbury Tales*, "The Miller's Tale" very specifically refers to a character getting up in the middle of the night, "risen for to pisse," and yep, it means exactly that. Dude had to wee. (Funny stuff happens from there, including farts and a hot iron to the "ers," and you should already know what that is. Give it a read if you haven't.)

So we know, right out, that it's at least as old as the fourteenth century, when Chaucer wrote the book. In fact, *pissen* was a decently common Middle English term, and not even all that rude. It's believed to have come from an Old French word, *pissier*, which itself was borrowed from Latin, but not the traditional, Classical Latin.

There were actually two kinds of Latin: the written word (Classical Latin), which we still have extant copies of now, and the dialectical, non-standard, spoken Latin, referred to as "Vulgar Latin," and not because they had words like *pissio,* which meant, well, piss. It's the more traditional form of vulgar, meaning "common" or "ordinary" instead of dirty (which makes it an auto-antonym as well!). It's like how we consider conversational English to be a bit looser than written English today.

As for where the Romans got it, the answer appears to be simple ono-matopoeia. Peeing makes kind of a "psss" noise when you really get right down to it, so those crude old Romans turned it into *pissio* because they knew how to party, and that involved a *lot* of wine, and that kind of explains everything, doesn't it?

2. F*ck

If there's any word in the English language that has more misinformation spread about its etymology, it's the *f*-word. From vague backronyms to out-right crap stories about "plucking yew," it's a freaking messy minefield that kind of makes you want to scream a certain four-letter word, right?

Let's knock those out right away: It's not an acronym for anything and never has been. For Unlawful Carnal Knowledge, Fornicating Under Con-sent of the King, and whatever else you've heard are all total urban legends. As for it coming from French archers who managed to not get their fingers cut off, come on. That story is way too ridiculous to be anything more than an overwrought joke.

Although the word was exceptionally taboo until recently (and it's still considered to be one of the worst now) and banned in print, it does still pop up here and there throughout the centuries. Perhaps the oldest usage is in an anonymous fifteenth-century faux-Latin poem called "Flen flyys," which includes a line that reads, "*Non sunt in coeli, quia gxddbov xxkxzt pg ifmk.*" That last part isn't in alien, but is actually encoded with a simple cipher. The line should really read: "*Non sunt in coeli, quia fvccant vvivys of heli.*"

When "translated," the line reads "They [meaning the monks the poem is mocking] are not in heaven because they f--k the wives of Ely," with *fvccant* being an attempted Latinization of ye olde *f*-bomb. Those are some pretty harsh words for a time when religion still reigned supreme, which is probably why it got encoded and was written anonymously.

Of course, it didn't just pop up overnight like that. Scholars believe the word probably developed from Germanic due to similar words like *fukka* in Norwegian, *fokka* in Swedish, *fokken* in Dutch, and *ficken* in German. As to where they all got it, that's where things get a little murkier, but it's possible that it's just a slang term that arose from Proto-German, which had the root word *fuk-*, meaning "to strike," which itself probably came from our old buddy Proto-Indo-European, whose root word *pug-* (also meaning "to strike") may be the origin, as well as definitely being the start of the Latin word *pugnis*, which meant "fist" (we are not talking about *that*, thank you). Now how's that for a f*cking history lesson?

1. ▪ C*nt

Whoa, the *c*-word. The big nasty. In the modern era, it's quickly overtaking the *f*-word as the rudest thing you can call someone (especially ladies) now that the latter has gotten tame enough that you can toss one into a PG-13 movie (occasionally two, or even three). Funny enough, however, both words actually have very similar etymologies.

In Middle English, the word existed much as it did today, but instead had spellings like *coynte* and *queynte*. In fact, before about the thirteenth century or so, see-you-next-Tuesday wasn't a bad word at all but was essentially an innocuous, straightforward word for vagina or vulva. It became slightly naughty by Chaucer's time, and by Shakespeare's it was pretty offensive, but for a long time it wasn't much worse than "hoo-hah."

Prior to its appearance in Middle English, it showed up in several Germanic languages, such as *kunta* in Swedish, *kott* and *kotze* in various forms of German, and *kont* in Dutch. Much like the *f*-word, though, beyond that things get hazy. One of two proposed Proto-Indo-European root words include *gon-,* which means "create" and is seen in modern words like "genital" and "gonad" (high-five if you just giggled at gonad like we did).

The other possible PIE origin is the root *gwneh-,* which means "woman" and can be seen in words like "gynecologist." It may also be responsible for the similar Latin word, *cunnus,* which just meant woman normally, but could also be used for exactly what you think it could, and that version was quite offensive then, too (they had more appropriate terms like, well, *vagina* and *vulva,* which is where we get them). In spite of the similarities, *cunnus* has not yet been established as being directly, etymologically linked to the big C, however.

The Ten Most Common English Names in Movies

It sure seems like movies are kind of samey these days. The blockbuster formula doesn't allow many deviations from the norm, unfortunately. As if it weren't enough that the actors and plots in movies were interchangeable, it turns out that the character names are as well. Some names just keep turning up in movies over and over again.

Does Hollywood not trust us with more unusual names, or are we just secretly more receptive to characters who are called familiar things and they know that? Whatever the reason, we might as well get used to seeing more and more characters with names like these.

The Numbers, a box office analysis website, took their database of 80,000 movie credits and picked out the most commonly recurring character names, which we're going to compare to the popularity of real-life baby names over the last 100 years (as determined by the U.S. Social Security Administration), just to see how well Hollywood's doing.

Male Names

It's been pretty well established that male characters make up the bulk of, well, basically everything in entertainment, despite only being 50 percent of the population. Four of the following five are more popular than *any* female name, which is kind of crazy.

We'll put that whole debate to bed for right now, though. What's more shocking is that *none of these names is Frodo.* That was a character's name in at least four movies we can think of. Is . . . is that not a lot?

5. ■ Frank

Bringing up the rear (although still extremely popular), and the only male name to not surpass every single female name in terms of popularity, is Frank. You've seen it in movies like *The Departed* (Frank Costello), *The Punisher* movies (Frank Castle), *Donnie Darko* (Frank the Bunny), and *The Transporter* series (Frank Martin).

To be frank (hah), Frank hasn't even been in the top five of actual baby names at any point in the last 100 years, according to the Social Security Administration. It hasn't even been in the top ten since 1922. Frankly (get it?), we find it really weird that Hollywood keeps going back to it, especially since it's currently around 300th in real-life popularity.

4. ■ John

Next up is a name that's synonymous with a toilet, and we aren't just saying that because we hate a couple of people with the name. You can find Johns in *The Terminator* series (John Connor), the *Die Hard* series (John McClane), every Sherlock Holmes adaptation (John Watson), and too many John Smiths to ever count.

Unlike Frank, John actually has been very popular among real people. It was number one from 1912 to 1923. After that, it still stayed in the top ten until 1986, and even dipped back into it in 1991. In the last few years it's hovered around number twenty-five, which makes it the only male name on this list that's actually still popular.

3. Paul

Well, if we can get George and Ringo in here we'll have a whole band. The Beach Boys, or The Monkees, or something. One of those. Anyway, Paul is used in *Misery* (Paul Sheldon), *American Psycho* (Paul Allen), *Zodiac* (Paul Avery), and the alien in the self-titled movie *Paul* (the one voiced by Seth Rogen). Okay, so those are mostly violent movies based on books, but hey, they're popular.

Paul has never been in the top ten baby names, according to the SSA, but it was pretty steadily popular in the mid-teens until the '70s. Since then, it has slowly dropped to its current ranking, close to number 200. So it's less popular than John as a baby name, but more popular as a movie name (presumably due to minor characters using it more than main ones, since most of the ones we found were small characters). So, uh, way to take a step backwards, Hollywood.

2. Sam

To be fair to this one, Sam can be both a male and female name, which may be bumping it up in the rankings a little, but it's quite popular regardless. You can find Sams in the *Transformers* movies (Sam Witwicky), *Ghost* (Sam Wheat), *The Maltese Falcon* (Sam Spade), and *The Lord of the Rings* trilogy (Sam Gamgee—wait, all the hobbits *weren't* called Frodo?).

Sam has never even been close to the most popular name, starting out at number sixty-three in the early twentieth century and steadily falling (with a few very small rises) to nearly 500th place today. Where are we going with this, Hollywood? Are we going to see a rash of movie characters named Billingham?

1. Jack

Well, now that we're here, it's not much of a surprise, is it? There's probably a character named Jack in every movie ever. If a character isn't given a name, assume it's Jack and you'll look like a psychic. Captain Jack Sparrow, Jack Skellington, Jack Ryan, and, of course, Jack Torrance from *The Shining* are just a few of the trillions of Jacks in cinema.

Of all the names so far, Jack has had the most consistent popularity. Starting with the 1900s, Jack ranked in the mid-to-high twenties, dropping down into the teens in the 1930s. It then dropped through the 1960s to the 1990s, reaching a low of 175th place, but it's now come back into favor and hangs on at 45th. In the realm of movies, we like to think it's a title instead of a name, and they only give it to babies with appropriately chiseled jaws and manly physiques.

Female Names

So how about the ladies, then? We can't have this be a big sausage festival, after all. Sometimes there's just too much sausage and you have to eat it, by which we mean we didn't understand what a "sausage fest" was and now we have all this food and we're not quite sure what to do with it. We could give it to the homeless, but that sounds like way more effort than just eating it ourselves. Slowly. While crying.

Anyway, despite what you might believe from hearing other people talk, not all female characters in movies are just the names of the actresses playing them. For example, in *The Avengers*, she's Black Widow, not just "Scarlett Johansson in that hot leather suit." In fact, we've heard rumors that some movies occasionally have females playing actual roles and not just flitting around in their underwear or whatever, but that's probably just a myth.

5. Alice

A name most famous for the *Alice in Wonderland* series, which in turn inspired the most acid-trippy of psychedelic songs of the '60s. Who says the hippies never contributed anything worthwhile? You can find Alice all over the place, from the *Resident Evil* series (whose protagonist is apparently just "Alice"), the *Twilight* series (Alice Cullen), *The Brady Bunch* franchise (Alice Nelson), and even the *Friday the 13th* movies (the "final girl" from the first film, Alice Hardy).

Alice was an extremely popular name in the early years of the twentieth century, usually in the top ten, but then fell off until it saw a major turnaround in 1999, starting at 424th place and rapidly making its way to 142nd place as of 2011 (the most recent year available), making it the first name so far on this list that's actually becoming significantly more popular instead of less. We're kind of thinking this one may all be on Stephenie Meyer.

4. Claire

Considering that Claire derives from the Latin *clarus*, which means famous, maybe it's fate that it's the fourth most popular movie name. Or maybe it's just a nice name and people like it, whichever. Claire has been used in movies like *The Breakfast Club* (Claire Standish), *Elizabethtown* (Claire Colburn), the *Resident Evil* movies again (Claire Redfield), and *Where the Wild Things Are* (just Claire).

Unlike Alice, Claire started out as a less popular name, ranking in the 200s, until the 1920s, when it saw a surge of use (probably due to flapper icon Clara Bow). Afterward, it sank down into the 500s before seeing another resurgence in the 1980s, which has continued to the present day, leaving it currently at number fifty, the most popular it's ever been. We're starting to think Hollywood has a better knack for girls' names than names of boys.

3. Lucy

It's not just Charlie Brown's "friend" Lucy (who does have a last name—Van Pelt—if you've ever wondered) who ended up with this name. It's surprisingly popular in the entertainment world, popping up in *The Chronicles of Narnia* series (Lucy Pevensie), all the various iterations of *Dracula* (Lucy Westenra/Weston/etc.), *50 First Dates* (Lucy Whitmore), and *Across the Universe* (just Lucy).

Lucy was fairly popular in the early twentieth century, hovering around number seventy-five. After that, however, it perpetually dropped like a rock until 1978, where it turned around from a low of 588 and has been trending upward ever since, right back to around number seventy-five again, as it happens. Hollywood, are you . . . *doing something right*? This is quite shocking.

2. Mary

The first name of every Catholic girl you've ever met (it may have something to do with that one that's in all their art?) is, naturally, extremely popular in movies. You can find women named Mary in the *Spider-Man* movies (Mary Jane Watson), *The Godfather Part III* (Mary Corleone, disastrously played by Sofia Coppola), *There's Something About Mary* (duh), and *Mary Poppins* (double duh).

Mary is, by far, the most popular name for real-life babies on this list, male or female. For nearly *sixty freaking years* it was the most popular girl's name, as in it was number one for basically that entire time (very occasion-ally dropping into the number two spot). It dropped a little afterward, into the twenties and thirties in the 1970s and '80s, before hitting the fifties in the 90s. Bummer. Since 2000, though, something weird has happened and the bottom has dropped out, taking it down to 112th place. Still, that's pretty recent movement, so we'll give Hollywood a pass and say they got another one right.

1. Sarah

So here we are, the most popular female name in moviedom, and it's also the name of every first-grade teacher ever (which is actually evidence of a mass conspiracy that proves we all have implanted memories, but we'll leave that for now). If you want to find Sarahs in popular movies, look no further than *The Terminator* series again (Sarah Connor), *Labyrinth* (Sarah Williams), *The Prestige* (Sarah Borden), and *Philadelphia* (Sarah Beckett).

Unlike most of the other names on this list, Sarah's popularity has remained pretty steady for the last hundred years, starting in the forties in the 1900s and dropping very slowly to a low of 119 in 1959. It then jumped into the top ten between 1978 and 2002 before declining back to number 39 as of 2011, and most of that drop has only occurred since 2007.

Hollywood, you are officially much wiser about choosing female names than male ones. Once we get some more Jacobs, Michaels, and Christophers in the mix, we can talk again. But you're not allowed to look us in the eye because you guys have mind powers and stuff. Deal?

Acknowledgments

I know, acknowledgments are so gauche in this day and age, but it's my book.

I'd like to thank Kathy Benjamin for recommending me for this book. I owe you, like, everything ever. Plus a puppy or something. Okay, ten puppies.

A massive, enormous thank you to all the people at Adams Media, especially Halli Melnitsky, who put up with my constant e-mails and weird questions.

I am in tremendous debt to the amazing editors, staff, and fellow writers at Cracked.com. That goes double to Jack O'Brien and David Wong for creating the Cracked Comedy Workshop, which is the best resource for any new writer on the Internet. It helped me build my writing career from scratch, no lie.

Also, a huge thanks to Jason English and the rest of the *Mental Floss* staff, Scott Beggs and Neil Miller at FilmSchoolRejects.com, and Adam Tod Brown (then at *Playboy*, now at Cracked.com) for all taking a chance on me and letting me make whole new audiences of people vaguely uncomfortable.

Finally, the biggest thanks of all to my family and friends, my wife, Alicia, and, of course, my mom and dad.

Oh, and I suppose I owe a weird thanks to the imaginary writing staff I came up with to be the voice of this book. I have no idea where they came from (probably from too many *Cracked* articles), but I'll take 'em.

Index

About the Author

ASHER CANTRELL is a freelance writer from Nashville, Tennessee, and the creator of *Weird Sh*t Blog*. His work has appeared in Cracked.com, *Mental Floss*, *Film School Rejects*, and *Playboy*'s *The Smoking Jacket*. He lives in a too-small apartment just outside of Nashville, with a Fel-Beast from the Endless Depths (commonly known as a cat) named Biscuit.